P9-AOG-031

05724

STAND PRICE
$ 5.00

The Language of
PAINTING

AN INFORMAL DICTIONARY

The Language of
PAINTING

AN INFORMAL DICTIONARY

WRITTEN AND ILLUSTRATED BY

JOHN N. BARRON

THE WORLD PUBLISHING COMPANY

CLEVELAND AND NEW YORK

Published by The World Publishing Company
2231 West 110th Street, Cleveland, Ohio 44102
Published simultaneously in Canada by Nelson, Foster & Scott Ltd.
First Printing 1967
Library of Congress Catalog Card Number: 67-21388
Printed in the United States of America

*"In art, there is only one thing worth while
and that is what cannot be explained."*
GEORGES BRAQUE

PREFACE

As the title of this volume indicates, the words contained herein have been limited to those pertinent to painting. They are restricted to those applying to Western painting, with such brief historical background as is relevant. The entries are of three basic types: first, those that refer to the actual materials and techniques of painting; second, those terms that appear in art criticism, describing principles, personalities, movements, and schools of painting; and third, those miscellaneous words that relate to painting as a profession.

Although mention is made of contemporary synthetic resin paints and aqueous medium paints, the emphasis throughout is on painting in oil. Words of several meanings are presented with only the one that applies to painting. Dates are included wherever I feel they are sufficiently informative. The article is sometimes added to a term, especially in the foreign version, when it is used as a title, or by reason of common usage. Usage also dictates the spelling of certain words—whether or not they are left in their original form or translated. The pronunciation guide, when given, is necessarily only approximate. As for cross-references, the reader is encouraged to look elsewhere in the book for any terms within the text of an entry about which he may wish to know more. The cross-references that I sometimes make at the end of an entry are often only additional suggestions, especially when worded "See also. . . ."

Delacroix once wrote that a dictionary is not a book, but an instrument, a tool; I have attempted to approach this dictionary in such a practical way. It is my hope that it may prove of use as a working grammar of the words of painting and as a handbook of reference for anyone—artist or amateur—whose interests include painting. I also hope that the presentation of these terms may serve to increase the understanding and appreciation of the painter and his work.

JOHN N. BARRON
New York City
January 1967

A

ABSORBENT GROUND. A ground that absorbs the medium from the paint, rendering it quick drying and leaving the surface without gloss. Usually it is a water base chalk mixture used on a panel. See *Ground*.

ABSTRACT. Non-representational, or non-figurative. Not depicting any recognizable visual object. Usually pertains to geometric shapes, but is sometimes applied to embryonic forms or even amorphous creations.

ABSTRACT EXPRESSIONISM. A movement in abstract painting that relies on a spontaneous intuitive approach, with emphasis on the act of painting rather than the result. A reaffirmation of the physical activity in creating a painting often resulting in a dramatization of the accidentals of drip, dribble, and splash. Became known as a school in New York City shortly after World War II. Also referred to as *Action Painting*.

ABSTRACTION. The term perhaps is relative. Actually, abstraction is present in all painting. The abstract elements of line, shape, color, and space are used in representing any recognizable concrete object—a tree—for instance. In addition, the tree is an abstraction as it is created on a two-dimensional surface, with paint, and not three-dimensionally, of wood. For purposes of verbal distinction, a painting of abstract, non-representational elements could be called pure abstraction.

ABSTRACT PAINTING. The significance of Abstract Painting lies in the presentation of the primary materials, principles, and methods of painting, rather than in the anecdotal or pictorial content. There is no intent to reproduce natural appearances, but to draw meaning from the subjective experience, or emotions, while denying the objective appearance of Nature that produced these emotions. Abstract Painting arose out of early Cubism, which still retained a representational element and developed into such related movements as Futurism, Orphism, Purism, and Synchromism.

ACADEMIC. Refers to the Academy—or the forces of tradition. Also implies the scholarly, historical approach, as well as being sometimes a synonym for the dull and pedantic. See *Academy*.

ACADEMY. An institution of art (not necessarily an organization of learning); typically a conservative, traditional, and officially recognized body formed to advance the arts along approved and established lines. The views of the academies are usually opposed by independent progressive artists. It is possible that when these individuals group together, however, they can form a more rigid association than that of the academicians. Examples of the academies are: the French Academy, founded in 1637; the Royal Academy of Arts in London, 1769; the American Academy of Arts and Sciences, 1780; National Academy of Design, 1825; American Academy in Rome, 1894; and the Amerian Academy of Arts and Letters in 1904.

ACETONE. A very powerful solvent, used in many commercial paint removers. It is highly flammable and should be employed with adequate ventilation. It mixes well with oils, water, and other solvents.

ACHROMATIC COLOR. Color without discernible hue. See *Color*.

ACRYLIC RESIN. See *Resin* and *Varnish.*

ACTION PAINTING. See *Abstract Expressionism.*

ADDITIVE COLOR MIXTURE. See *Color.*

ADULTERANT. An inert material added to pigments to produce a cheaper paint. See also *Extender.*

AEGEAN PAINTING. The term refers to the early painting of the geographic areas of the Aegean Sea, namely Crete and Greece. See *Greek Painting* and *Minoan Painting.*

AERIAL COMPOSITION. The term has been used to refer to a composition, the basis for which is a scene viewed from an elevated position or bird's-eye view. It implies a panorama with the use of a distant horizon and aerial perspective.

AERIAL PERSPECTIVE. A term that refers to the achievement of the illusion of spatial depth by atmospheric changes, as compared with linear perspective, which concerns itself with changes of size, form, and direction. Aerial perspective makes use of the principle that, as objects recede into space, their edges grow less distinct, their dark and light contrasts decrease, and their color intensities diminish. These latter change toward the blues or

An example of aerial perspective. (FROM MONET—*detail*)

cooler colors, due to the atmospheric moisture through which they are viewed, plus the light reflected from the blue of the sky. Both combine to form atmospheric color. See also *Color* and *Linear Perspective*.

AESTHETICS. (Also *Esthetics.*) A study of, and concern with, the beautiful in art, as distinguished from the moral and the useful. Theories and systems have developed, drawing from philosophy, psychology, psychiatry, cultural history, and the social sciences in an effort to form a science, with principles and laws, of the appreciation and creation of art. These theories vary considerably, depending upon their sources. Aesthetics is very much a matter of artistic criticism. Yet, the basic controversy has always been the subjective, or the intuitive, as a matter of "feeling" on the one hand, versus the objective, or the rational, with logical rules and principles on the other. In the first case, its proponents maintain that beauty depends upon the observer while, in the second, its adherents believe that beauty is in the object. Regardless of the viewpoint, to experience something aesthetically is to enjoy its beauty. This means to take pleasure from its quality as an object, excluding any symbolism of idea, belief, or concept—that is, as an object in itself. Works of art are not always created just to be enjoyed or to be experienced aesthetically, but they always will have aesthetic significance.

AFTERIMAGE. The term refers to the experiencing of a color sensation after the stimulus is no longer present. When the eye is exposed to an intense color until the receptors are fatigued (color fatigue) and then is shifted to a neutral or white background, the color perceived will be the complementary color of the original one. More exactly, this is sometimes called the negative afterimage. The positive afterimage would be evident when the eye is closed after being exposed to a brightly lighted image and the image is still seen. See also *Color*.

AGENT. A representative for the painter, primarily in his business affairs. See *Dealer.*

A.I.R. These letters mean "Artist in Residence." They are used on signs at entranceways of loft buildings to indicate to various city services that an artist has a living-working studio in a commercial building, and is so registered. See also *Artist-in-Residence.*

AIR BRUSH. A precision spraying device for paints, inks, etc. About the size of a fountain pen, and available in several different types, it is designed to throw a fine line as well as an area spray for work with friskets and stencils. Pressure is obtained through a light hose attached to a carbonic pressure tank, or to an air compressor of cylinder, diaphragm, or piston variety.

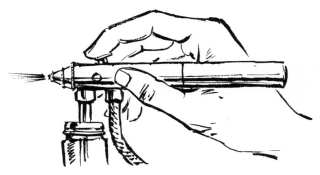

An air brush with jar attachment.

ALCOHOL. There are several different alcohols used as solvents and thinners. (1) The best grade of grain or ethyl alcohol is anhydrous ethyl alcohol and is water-free. This is available only to licensed commercial users. (2) Denatured alcohol is ethyl alcohol deliberately rendered unfit for drinking, and thereby for some solvent uses, by the addition of various materials; however, it can be used as a shellac thinner and sometimes as a varnish solvent.

(3) Wood alcohol (methyl alcohol), used to denature ethyl alcohol, is very poisonous as liquid and vapor and should be avoided.

ALIZARIN CRIMSON. (Alizarin Red, Alizarin Scarlet, Alizarin Lake.) A synthetic organic lake made from a coal-tar derivative. It replaces the natural madder lakes, which are considerably less permanent. Alizarin crimson in oil is somewhat transparent, of poor film quality, a slow dryer, and considered by some authorities to be not absolutely permanent. Yet, as a cool compatible red, it is necessary on the palette.

ALKYD RESIN. See *Resin.*

ALLA PRIMA (ah-lah PREE-mah). (It.) An expression that refers to the method of finishing a painting at one sitting, or at once. Also known as *Au Premier Coup.*

ALLIGATOR CRACKS. See *Cracks in Painting.*

ALUMINA HYDRATE. Artificially produced aluminum hydroxide. A fluffy, white powder, it is used widely as an extender, an inert base for lake colors.

AMATEUR. Formerly, an amateur was a lover of art who cultivated his interest for itself alone. Knowledgeable about painting, and in some cases actually producing pictures of considerable quality, he could be proud of the appellation. He was often a man of means on whom the professional artist relied for support, a role now played by the collector. Gradually, the term "amateur" has come to mean a dilettante, a dauber, as opposed to a professional, one skilled enough to sell his work.

AMBER. See *Resin.*

AMBIANCE. The totality of the surrounding and enhancing elements of a painting relative to the central idea. These would include the general color scheme, the con-

14

tributing movements, and the disposition of dark and light, pattern, and texture.

AMBIGUITY. While the word is used to describe general obscurity, it more often refers to the capability of a form or graphic visualization to be understood or interpreted in two (or more) different ways.

AMBIGUOUS SPACE. Space represented in such a way that it may be readily interpreted to exist either on the two-dimensional surface of the picture or in the picture's illusion of three-dimensional depth. Also, any similar equivocal relationship throughout the painting, such as the interpenetration of planes, etc. See also *Interpenetration* and *Space*.

AMORPHOUS. Without form; shapeless.

ANALOGOUS. A word indicating the resemblances in the function of certain elements in different paintings, and in the effect they produce. These elements can include color, shape, and line as well as space, weight, movement, etc. The comparison is made between these elements rather than between the paintings themselves.

ANALOGOUS COLOR. See *Color Wheel*.

ANALYTICAL CUBISM. See *Cubism*.

ANECDOTAL PAINTING. Illustrative painting in which a narrative incident is portrayed.

ANGST (ahngst). (Ger.) The term appears in art criticism when reference is made to the quality of anguish or anxiety as it affects the painter's personality and is expressed in his work.

ANGULAR PERSPECTIVE. See *Linear Perspective*.

ANILINE COLORS. Synthetic, organic dyes produced from aniline, a derivative of coal tar. Although useful in printing, etc., few have been judged permanent enough to be added as paints to the artist's palette.

ANIMAL GLUE. See *Glue*.

ANTHROPOMORPHIC FORM. Abstract form, obviously not human, to which human characteristics have been attributed or ascribed.

ANTWERP BLUE. See *Prussian Blue*.

APPEARANCE. The term refers to an object as seen, or as it appears to be, in contrast to its reality, or to the real.

AQUARELLE (ah-kwah-REL). (Fr.) A term used to describe water-color painting that makes use of the transparent quality of color over white paper or ground, thus distinguishing it from other water-color techniques which use opaque or body color.

Two examples of the arabesque: top, Arabic 14th century; bottom, copy of Renaissance Italian.

ARABESQUE (ah-rah-BESK). (Fr.) A flowery interlacing design involving scrolls, foliage, fruit, and sometimes birds, reptiles, and human forms. An arabesque can be flowing and linear or geometric in character. The arabesque in painting, therefore, pertains to decorative embellishment related to the above.

16

ARCHAIC. Pertains to an earlier or more primitive time, form, or style. Ancient or antiquated.

ARCHAICISM. A term referring to a use of the ancient or primitive qualities of style, etc., in contemporary painting. Also called *Primitivism*. See *Primitivism*.

ARCHITECTONIC. Structurally conceived, architecturally constructed design.

AREA. The term usually refers to the extent of a flat two-dimensional space on the surface of the canvas or picture plane.

ARMORY SHOW. An international exhibition of painting and sculpture organized by a group of progressive American painters and presented in the Armory of the 69th Regiment in New York in 1913. This was the first real look by America at the European (mainly French) artistic developments of the 19th and early 20th centuries. Included was the work of Cézanne, van Gogh, Gauguin, Picasso, Braque, Matisse, Rouault, Bonnard, Dufy, Léger, and Duchamps.

ART. Art is an interpretation and re-creation of the pattern of forces and the living processes of Nature. From the activity of this re-creation, the artist constructs a world with rules and laws, principles and methods that parallel those of the world of Nature. His world is an equivalent, not an imitation. Art is the result of this effort on the part of the artist to organize his experience of life, to communicate his awareness of it, and to express its meaning. In a sense, art is actually a by-product or record of the artist's activity in a state of awareness of, and receptivity to, those interrelationships between the world around him and his own inner world. Art is not an imitation of reality, but evidence of its discovery.

ART BRUT, L' (lahr BRIU). (Fr.)   The art of the insane, the uneducated, and of prisoners, clairvoyants, etc. As painting, it is crude, rough, and raw. Its champions cite its directness, power, and vitality. Certainly, in addition to its shock value, it has qualities not found in the safe, the proper, the decorative, and the precious.

ARTIST. A person who has the imagination, creative ability, and technical skill to produce art. The artist as painter sees, appreciates, and re-creates in the medium of paint significant interrelationships of basically visual quality. His conception and execution are governed by aesthetic judgment and originality. Through his work he gives an awareness to his experience of life. See also *Art* and *Painter*.

ARTISTE MAUDIT (ahr-TEEST moh-DEE). (Fr.) The image of the artist as accursed wretched.

Art nouveau poster of 1897.
(FROM MUCHA)

ARTIST-IN-RESIDENCE. An artist who arranges to live near a college or university and whose studio, either on campus or nearby, is open to certain students. The teaching involved is more of the nature of master and apprentice or of the seminar, rather than that of the usual classroom.

ART NOUVEAU (ahr noo-VOH). (Fr.) A decorative, curvilinear style based on the forms of Nature such as flowers and vines, goldfish, and peacocks. The movement originated in Belgium in the early 1890's, eventu-

18

ally spreading throughout Europe and to America. In Belgium, it was associated with *Les Vingt* (The XX); in Vienna, with the Sezessionists. In Germany, it was called "Jugendstil," and in Italy, "Stile Liberty." Although the style was ornamentally valid, it was never particularly related to the objects it attempted to decorate.

ASHCAN SCHOOL. A group of progressive and more or less socially conscious American painters who used, as subject matter, the contemporary everyday life (mainly urban) that they saw around them. In the early 1900's, this painting of the "American scene" was not particularly congenial to the prevalent artistic attitude and hence their name. The movement, of which Bellows was a member, grew from "The Eight": Henri, Luks, Glackens, Sloan, Shinn, Davies, Pendergast, and Lawson. Most were members of the Association of Painters and Sculptors who brought about the Armory Show. See *Armory Show.*

ASPHALTUM (Bitumen). A dark brown color made of asphalt or tar dissolved in oil and turpentine. Never dries, is impermanent, and causes wrinkling and cracking. It was the so-called "brown sauce" glaze of the 19th century, but is now absolutely avoided.

ASSEMBLAGE (ah-sahn-BLAHZH). (Fr.) See *Found Object.*

A-TECTONIC. Biomorphic or free form; loose open form; the opposite of tectonic. See also *Tectonic.*

ATELIER (ah-tel-YAY). (Fr.) A studio or workshop, either of an individual artist or of a school. See also *Studio.*

ATMOSPHERIC COLOR. See *Aerial Perspective.*

ATOMIZER. A device for spraying thin liquids such as fixative or thinned varnish. There is the simple mouth

19

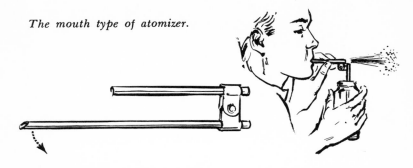

The mouth type of atomizer.

type of blower for light applications, and also the familiar bulb-squeezing type.

ATTENUATED FORM. A term used in criticism to describe the distortion of form toward thinness or meagerness as contrasted with the "fullness" of form.

AU PREMIER COUP (oh prehm-yay COO). (Fr.) An expression that refers to the method of finishing a painting at one sitting, literally "at the first blow." Also known as *Alla Prima*.

AUREOLIN. See *Cobalt Yellow*.

AUTOMATISM. A term used by the Surrealists to describe the subconscious aspects of creating a painting. See also *Surrealism*.

AVANT-GARDE (ah-vah*n*-GAHRD). (Fr.) During a particular period, the most daring and original of the innovators of ideas and techniques are considered the advance guard—the opposite of the *arrière-garde,* or that of the rear.

AXIS. All forms or volumes have basic cores, center lines of weight around which the mass is balanced. There is one principal axis, with often a secondary one at right angles to it. In simplified volumes or in two-dimensional planes, the axes are obvious, but in more complicated forms, they

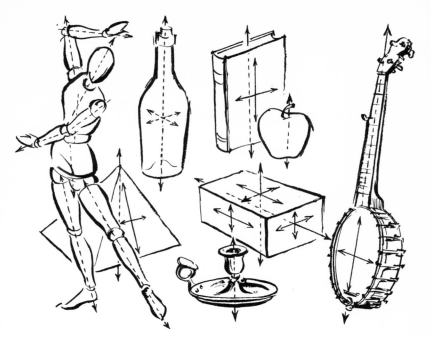

Examples of the axes of various volumes and planes.

must be sensed or felt. The principal axis through the center of the form is important in showing direction of the form's movement, and in the realization of tensions.

AZURE BLUE. Formerly meant a type of cobalt blue (smalt) that had replaced a blue made from copper. Now the term "azure" blue has come to mean any shade resembling "sky" blue.

B

BACKGROUND. In traditional painting, pictures are often divided into roughly three sections at progressive distance from the viewer. Foreground—that part closest

to the picture surface; middle distance; and background—
the farthest depth of space. This division is best illustrated
by the usual landscape. Background also can be the overall area or ground, seen or felt, upon which a closer object,
shape, or figure may exist. In this case, it is considered a
two-dimensional negative shape.

Symmetrical balance. (FROM TITIAN)

Asymmetrical balance. (LEFT FROM CÉZANNE, RIGHT FROM DEGAS)

BALANCE. Balance is one of the important basic principles of art. It is the equilibrium achieved when all the
contrasting visual forces of the pictorial space are resolved.
In a work of art, this equilibrium is dynamic, with opposing tensions actively compensating for each other. A
stability can result from the interaction of such factors as
weight, direction, location, shape, color, and psychological

interest. Balance is a means of achieving unity, increasing the power and clarity of the expressive statement, and producing a sense of universality or timelessness. (It duplicates in a painting the artist's—and the viewer's—striving for equilibrium in his life, and its value is in its ability to assist in the revealing of meaning or content.) Balance is a highly complex, dynamic arrangement in space. It cannot be objectively measured but it is best judged intuitively by the eye. However, the main factors that determine balance are recognized to be weight and direction.

A distinction can be made between symmetrical balance and asymmetrical balance. The former occurs in the vertically divided painting which contains corresponding elements of size, shape, or volume in each of its halves. Asymmetrical balance, however, is achieved through the juxtaposition of dissimilar elements such as space with volume, or open areas with detail, or through strong contrasts of movement. Absolute symmetrical balance or a mirror image, of course, is seldom employed. One factor affecting both symmetrical and asymmetrical balance is the usual tendency of the viewer to "lead into" a picture from the lower left corner, and thus give more weight to an object on the left side than the same object on the right. The sense of direction from left to right is stronger, or, in action, faster. The artist who has looked at his work in a mirror is aware of this occurrence and often attempts to compensate for it. This subtle inequality in directional speed or weight has been attributed to our Occidental manner of reading from left to right. See also *Direction* and *Weight*.

BALSAM. See *Oleoresin.*

BARBIZON SCHOOL. A group of landscape painters who left Paris and gathered in 1830 in Barbizon, a small village on the edge of the forest of Fontainebleau. They had reacted against the Classical Italianate landscape and believed in a fresh direct look at the actualities of Nature. Included in the group were Theodore Rousseau, Millet, Corot, Daubigny, Diaz, and Troyon. Their work influenced American painting, especially that of Inness. The ideas of the Barbizon painters lead into French Realism and Impressionism.

BARIUM YELLOW. A pale cool yellow made of barium chromate. Sometimes called lemon yellow. As it is slightly poisonous and is said by some authorities to assume a greenish cast, it is best replaced by other yellows, such as the lighter cadmiums.

BAROQUE. Growing from the decorative motifs of the Classical ornament in late 16th-century Italy, the Baroque was a 17th-century modification of Renaissance styles and a reaction against Mannerism, which had distorted the rationality of the Late Renaissance. It was produced by the Counter Reformation devoted to the exaltation of religion and the new aristocracy. The Baroque was somewhat theatrical, restless, and characterized by a sense of "becoming" or endlessness, rather than the Classical "being." Baroque painters had an excited interest in the careful observation of the natural world and as a result invited the viewer to participate in their observation. The Baroque developed into the Rococo. In Italy, the work of the painter Caravaggio (1573–1610) is illustrative of the Baroque style. In the North, the paintings of Rubens (1577–1640), Poussin (1594–1665), and the early Rembrandt (1606–1669), and in Spain, those of El Greco (1541–1614) are among the many examples.

BASE. An inert material that has been dyed or stained to form a pigment known as a lake. See also *Pigments*.

BAUHAUS. An outgrowth of the Academy of Arts and Crafts, the Bauhaus was a school of design founded by

Walter Gropius in Weimar, Germany, in 1919. Under a staff that included leading architects, painters, and sculptors, the Bauhaus grew to be a focal point of the progressive trends in art for industry. In 1925, the school was moved to Dessau into new buildings, which were designed by Gropius and were outstanding examples of the International Style. The direct influence of the Bauhaus on industrial design and architecture continued until it was closed by the Nazis in 1933.

BEATNIK. See *Bohemian*.

BEAUTY. Beauty has been defined as the quality of giving pleasure to the senses, the mind, and/or the spirit. Beauty is "pleasure objectified," or the quality of being aesthetically pleasing. In painting, the visual sense is obviously the prime receptor. Standards of beauty vary with cultures, periods, and social groups. In individuals, beauty is a matter of taste and opinion, therefore ambiguous. See also *Aesthetics*.

BEAUX-ARTS (boh-ZAHR). (Fr.)   The fine arts.

BEESWAX. In its white refined form, beeswax is the usual wax used in the artist's various wax recipes and processes. It is the principal ingredient in the medium used in hot-wax or encaustic painting. It is added to oil paints to give them a proper buttery consistency, and it has been used as a final protective coat on oil paintings, either alone or mixed with varnishes. In relining and mounting pictures, beeswax is used in the nonaqueous adhesive.

BEIGE. Not an exact color, but one resembling the natural color of unbleached cotton or wool.

BELLE ÉPOQUE, La (lah bel eh-PAWK). (Fr.)   "The Beautiful Period," in France, approximating the time between the end of the Franco-Prussian War in 1871 and the start of World War I in 1914.

BELLE PEINTURE (bel pan-TYOOR). (Fr.) "Beautiful Painting." Refers to an obvious love of the materials, an enjoyment of the qualities of the medium by the painter. This is evidenced in the painting by sensuous paint handling, brush work, etc. The term is also used to differentiate easel painting from other less intimate forms of painting such as mural painting. See also *Paint Quality*.

BENZENE (Benzol). A highly poisonous and powerful solvent distilled from coal tar. It is found in some paint removers and brush cleaners and is used as a rubber cement thinner. Highly flammable. Not to be confused with the petroleum solvent, *benzine*.

BENZINE. A petroleum solvent less volatile than gasoline, but more volatile than mineral spirits. Also called V.M. and P. Naphtha. Not to be confused with *benzene*.

BENZOL. See *Benzene*.

BERLIN BLUE. See *Prussian Blue*.

BIANCO SANGIOVANNI (bee-AHN-co sahn-joh-VAH-nee). (It.) A white pigment used in fresco painting, made of calcium hydroxide and calcium carbonate.

BICE. Several types of blue pigments made from poisonous copper compounds. They are impermanent and no longer used.

BINDER. Generally speaking, anything in the painting medium that binds together the particles of pigment adhesively and holds them onto their support. In oil painting, binders are drying oils that form tough adhesive films. Binders are to be distinguished from thinners, which merely dilute and extend the paint to facilitate its manipulation. In water-color techniques, the binders are various gums and glues. See *Drying Oil*.

26

BIOMORPHIC. Free form; shaped in a vital way as in a living form. Opposed to tectonic or geometric.

BISTRE. A light brownish color made from soot obtained by charring wood; applied in washes and inks. Impermanent and seldom used.

BITUMEN. See *Asphaltum*.

BLANC FIXE (blah*n* FEEKS). (Fr.) Artificial barium sulphate. It is used as a permanent white in fresco painting, and as an extender or base for the more opaque lake colors.

BLAUE REITER, Der (der BLOU-uh RYE-ter). (Ger.) "The Blue Rider." Started as a magazine by Marc and Kandinsky, *Der Blaue Reiter* became the name under which a group of German painters exhibited together, starting in Munich in 1912. Also included were Klee, Mäcke, and Münter, as well as contemporary artists from France, Russia, etc. Generally, these artists experimented with the intense, complementary colors of Fauvism in a somewhat geometrical, Cubist style. See *Fauvism*.

BLEEDING. The objectionable ability of certain pigments of the dye or stain variety to penetrate or "strike through" an overlaying layer of paint, or to stain an adjoining area.

BLOCK-IN. To indicate loosely on the canvas the principal objects and/or figures, etc. in the form of simplified masses or volumes. See also *Lay-In*.

BLOOM. A coat of varnish is said to bloom or to have bloom when it dries with a blue-white mistiness instead of a clear transparency. This is due to moisture (picked up from the atmosphere or from improper mixture) trapped in the varnish. Certain varnishes, such as dammar, seem less susceptible to blooming than others.

BLOW-UP. To enlarge by projection. Also the result of such enlargement. (The term is taken from photography.)

BLUE RIDER, The. See *Blaue Reiter, Der.*

BODY COLOR. Opaque, comparatively heavy paint that gains its paler tints from an admixture of opaque white. As opposed to a glaze or, in speaking of transparent watercolor techniques, *aquarelle.*

BOHEMIAN. Originally meant a gypsy from Bohemia, a province of western Czechoslovakia, but now used to describe an artist, a nonconformist, etc., who leads a life in protest against, or indifferent to, the accepted conventions of society. (The word may well be superseded by "beatnik.")

BOILED OIL. See *Linseed Oil.*

BOLE. A pigment, white, green, or more usually red, which is mixed with glue size and applied as a ground for gold leaf. Native earth colors are used, especially the red oxides. In painting, grounds toned with Armenian bole or Venetian red are called *Bolus Grounds.* See also *Gilding.*

BOLUS GROUND. A ground toned with bole, a native red oxide. See also *Bole.*

BONE BLACK. See *Ivory Black.*

BRAVURA. (It.) A term taken from music and used in art criticism to indicate a painter's brilliant, daring style or performance.

BRIDGE, The. See *Brücke, Die.*

BRISTOL BOARD. Used in general commercial art work, it is made of at least two sheets (2-ply) of heavy paper glued together. Available in various weights and surfaces. The best is of 100 per cent rag content.

BROKEN COLOR. Color applied in patches of different value or hue, often over an under painting of a different color. The opposite of flat color or smoothly modulated color.

BRUCKE, Die (dee BREHK-uh). (Ger.) "The Bridge." A group of German painters whose work derived from and paralleled Fauvism. Starting in Dresden in 1905, the group was composed of Nolde, Kirchner, Heckel, Schmidt-Rottluff, Bleyl, and Pechstein. Later, when the painters moved to Berlin, their work became more expressionistic. See also *Expressionism.*

BRUSHES. Since ancient times, brushes have been used by the painter in practically their present form. With the exception of the Egyptian frayed reed brush, they have always been made of animal hair fastened to a handle. In smaller brushes, quills were used (and occasionally are still used) to connect the glued-together hair with the handle. During the last century, the metal ferrule has been used for this purpose. Depending upon the medium used, and personal preference, the modern painter will use any of the following brushes:

Badger. Usually called the badger "blender." This brush has the same hair as a shaving brush with a somewhat flattened, spread-out shape. Formerly used much more than now to smooth out or blend the transitions between colors.

Blender. See *Badger.*

Brights. Short flat brushes with long handles. See *Bristle.*

Bristle. The bristle brush is the standard brush for paint-

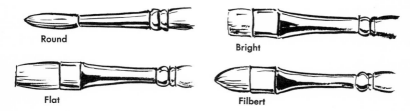

Bristle brushes.

29

ing in oil. Bristle brushes are made from selected bleached white hogs' bristles fastened by a metal ferrule to a long round wooden handle. The tip of the brush must be the natural end of the bristles, which are split at the tip. A good brush makes use of the natural curve of some bristles to counteract any tendency of the brush to spread. Brushes are available in bristles of different lengths in about a dozen sizes and in a variety of shapes:

(1) Rounds: These are completely round and set in a rounded ferrule. They vary from a fairly sharp to a blunt point. They are similar to those used by the old masters, and are especially useful in linear work.

(2) Flats: More versatile, they have an oblong shape with a flat edge, and are set in a flattened ferrule.

(3) Brights: Similar to flats, but thinner and shorter, about half as long.

(4) Filberts: Similar to flats, set in a flattened ferrule, but somewhat rounded at their end.

Camel hair. Actually made of squirrel hair, and used mainly in water-color techniques, they are very soft and have little life or spring. Among the cheapest of brushes.

Cutters. Flat bristle brushes with their edges cut on an angle, used by sign painters.

Fan. Available in bristle or sable, they are used in glazing and blending, etc. They have a fanlike, spread-out shape.

Filberts. Flat brushes with rounded points and long handles. See *Bristle*.

Fitches. Bristle brushes with a natural square chiseled edge, used by lettering men and sign painters.

Flats. Oblong-shaped flat brushes with long handles. See *Bristle*.

Glazing. Any of several broad soft brushes, either in bristle or sable. See *Badger* and *Fan*.

Lettering. Principally made in sable or camel hair. Whether in round or flat ferrules, lettering brushes are

30

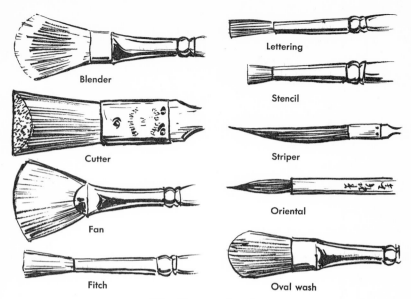

Blender

Lettering

Cutter

Stencil

Fan

Striper

Fitch

Oriental

Oval wash

Miscellaneous brushes.

always cupped to give a square, straight edge. They are also sometimes called *riggers,* and are used in lettering and, in large sizes, in water color.

Liners. Pointed, long-haired sable or camel hair brushes for ornamental linear work.

Nylon. Used in general painting purposes and set in the conventional short flat handle.

Oil. The principal oil brushes are bristles and sables, all with long handles. See *Bristle* and *Sable.*

Oriental. Mounted in bamboo handles, these soft flexible brushes are usually made of squirrel hair. Used in water color, and wash and ink drawings, they hold much liquid and come to an extremely fine and delicate point.

Oval-filbert brushes. See *Bristle.*

Ox hair. With somewhat more spring than sable, and slightly stiffer like bristle, ox hair is used as a cheaper substitute, especially in larger sizes.

Riggers. See *Lettering.*

Sable brushes.

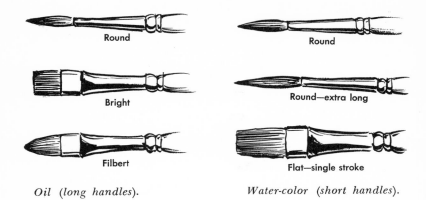

Round

Round

Bright

Round—extra long

Filbert

Flat—single stroke

Oil (long handles).   *Water-color (short handles).*

Rounds. Round brushes with long handles. See *Bristle.*
Sable. The best and true red sable brushes are made of
the hairs from the tail of the Kolinsky or Siberian mink.
This hair is especially springy and tough and tapers to a
fine point. The tip of the brush is the natural end of the
hair and not trimmed. Sable brushes with short handles
are used extensively in water color; with long handles, in
oil, tempera, casein, etc., for smooth, fine, or delicate work.
The water-color brushes are available in about a dozen
sizes of rounds with fine points, and in different lengths
of hair, as well as flats or single-stroke brushes. The oil
brushes are available as rounds, brights (short and flat),
and filberts (flat with rounded point).
Single-stroke (or one-stroke brushes). Used in lettering
and water color, they are flat and available in sable or
ox hair.
Stencil. Round brushes of varying diameter, with bristles
cut off square and set in short handles, they are used
for stencil work.
Stripers. The dagger striper is a long full flat brush with
a slanting edge used to give a clean even line.

Tempera. Usually round pointed sable brushes are used with tempera, and the paint is applied in single, individual strokes.

Varnish. Wide flat nonshedding brush of either bristle or ox hair.

Wash. Any large, flat, rounded tip brush used for washes, skies, etc., in water color can be called a wash brush.

Water-color. Usually with shorter handles, the best water-color brushes are made of sable hair. Others are made of ox hair, squirrel hair, etc. See *Sable*.

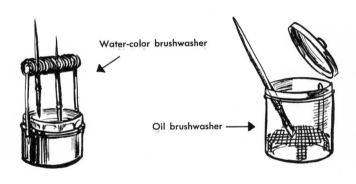

Water-color brushwasher

Oil brushwasher ➤

BRUSHWASHER. (1) A metal water container with a spiral wire fastened above it used to hold water-color brushes in a vertical, tip-down position. (2) An oil brush cleaner in the form of a covered tin container enclosing a wire mesh, which is set a few inches above the bottom. To clean the brushes, they are scrubbed against this false bottom in turpentine (which, as the pigment settles, can be used repeatedly).

BRUSHWORK. Refers to the handling of paint as evidenced in the brush strokes. This involves their general character, size, direction, speed, and pressure on the support. There can be a great variety of strokes; smooth and flowing, strong and spontaneous, slow and hesitant, scrubbed, dabbed or flicked. They exist as the personal "handwriting" of the individual artist. Certain contemporary schools of painting make brushwork and the application of paint ends in themselves. See *Paint Quality*.

BUON FRESCO. See *Fresco*.

BURLAP. Used as a fabric for a painting support. Generally of coarse weave, and impermanent when made of jute or hemp. See *Canvas*.

BURNT GREEN EARTH. A natural earth color that has been roasted. It is a deep, transparent brown color. See also *Green Earth*.

BURNT SIENNA. A natural earth color (raw sienna) that has been roasted. It is a permanent, very useful, fiery orange-red, and has been known since ancient times.

BURNT UMBER. A natural earth color (raw umber) that has been roasted. It is a permanent, very useful, quick drying, dark red-brown, and has been known since ancient times.

BYZANTINE ART. The Eastern Roman, or Byzantine Empire, was centered at Byzantium, renamed Constantinople by Emperor Constantine I (A.D. 330), and made the capital of the entire Roman Empire. (The modern city is Istanbul.) Byzantine Art was a mixture of Greek and Oriental traditions and reached the First Golden Age c. 330, which culminated in a characteristic Byzantine Art. In the 8th century and part of the 9th, there occurred the Iconoclastic Controversy during which all artistic representation of sacred personages was banned. This action drove many artists to emigrate to Italy and France, spreading the Byzantine influences in Pre-Renaissance Europe. In the next period during the 10th and 12th centuries when religious painting was again encouraged, Byzantine art reached its climax in the Second Golden Age under the Macedonian dynasty. This period lasted until the sack of Constantinople in 1204. The final period was a general decline, lasting from the restoration until the fall of Constantinople to the Turks in 1453. The Byzantine style is exemplified in mosaics, frescoes, wood panels known as icons, and in the miniatures in manuscripts. It is characterized by a distortion of proportions, a formal art of Oriental decoration and ornamentation unified in shallow space compositions by linear decorative patterns.

C

CABINET PICTURE. A term that is occasionally employed to describe a small easel painting, usually of an interior or a still life, used as a decorative object on the wall.

CADMIUM-BARIUM PIGMENTS. See *Cadmium Pigments.*

CADMIUM ORANGE. See *Cadmium Pigments.*

CADMIUM PIGMENTS. These artificially produced mineral pigments are made in a range of colors from pale yellows through brilliant oranges to deep reds. The yellows and oranges are cadmium sulphide; the reds have an addition of cadmium selenide. Many of the cadmium pigments also have the addition of barium sulphate. They are then correctly called *cadmium-barium pigments,* and are slightly weaker in tinting power. Both varieties are permanent, opaque, and extremely useful.

CADMIUM RED. See *Cadmium Pigments.*

CADMIUM YELLOW. See *Cadmium Pigments.*

CALCIUM CARBONATE. See *Chalk* and *Whiting*.

CALLIGRAPHIC. The term describes a linear quality in the nature of handwriting. Anything from elegant flowing lines to spontaneous marks that derive from accidental movements of the brush may be termed calligraphic.

CAMAÏEU (kah-mah-ee-YIU). (Fr.) Painting in a single color. See *Monochrome*.

CAMDEN TOWN GROUP. The name given to a group of painters in England who formed an association in 1911, under the influences of Post-Impressionist French painting, and who exhibited together for a few years. Included were such painters as Walter Sickert (1860–1942), Augustus John (1878–1961), and Lucien Pissarro (1863–1944). The organization merged in 1913 to form the London Group.

CAMERA LUCIDA. A precision-made mechanical instrument of a few inches in length having a prism and a series of lenses. It makes possible the accurate copying, enlarging, and reducing of any object, scene, or two-dimensional drawing, photograph, or painting.

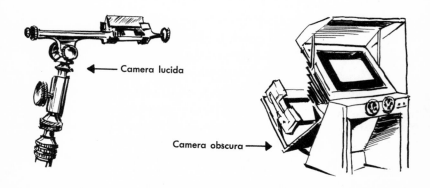

← Camera lucida

Camera obscura →

CAMERA OBSCURA. A darkened closet or large box having an aperture, equipped with a lens, through which the light rays from an object or scene enter. These reproduce an image on the opposite surface, or on a glass, where it can be traced off. The modern versions are developed from those of the 16th century. The photographic camera may be said to be a modern form of the camera obscura.

CAMP. A revived form of *Art Nouveau*, characterized by affectation or pretentiousness, often associated with extreme fashion.

CANADA BALSAM. See *Oleoresin*.

CANVAS. The fabric upon which the artist paints. Canvas may be made from closely woven jute, hemp, cotton, or linen. Of these, jute and hemp are unsatisfactory, mainly because they age quickly. Cotton is a serviceable textile but considerably inferior to linen. The best canvas is pure linen (made from the fibers of the flax plant), tightly woven with warp and woof threads of equal weight. Until the end of the 18th century, canvas was woven by hand, giving it a varied and interesting surface texture. Many artists prepare or prime their canvas themselves for a surface of more individual character; this also gives them control over quality at an economical price. Canvas is primed with glue size and one or two coats of ground, after being stretched on a frame of stretcher strips. At this stage, the term *canvas* refers to the individual support. See also *Ground*.

CANVAS BOARD. Cardboard, onto which prepared canvas has been glued. Canvas board purchased in art stores is generally highly absorbent and of variable quality; however, it is perfectly reliable when made of good canvas attached to a more permanent panel, such as Presdwood.

CANVAS PINS. Double-pointed pins in a wood base that are used to hold apart freshly painted canvases while they are being transported.

CANVAS SEPARATOR CLIPS. Strong spring-controlled clips that are used in carrying two freshly painted canvases face to face.

CANVAS SIZES, French. French canvases are classified as "Portrait" or "Landscape," and are in several numbered sizes; the most usual are given below—height before width.

NO.	PORTRAIT	LANDSCAPE
#15	65 cm x 54 cm $25\frac{1}{2}''$ x $21\frac{1}{4}''$	50 cm x 65 cm $19\frac{1}{2}''$ x $25\frac{1}{2}''$
#20	73 cm x 60 cm $28\frac{1}{2}''$ x $23\frac{1}{2}''$	54 cm x 73 cm $21\frac{1}{4}''$ x $28\frac{1}{2}''$
#25	81 cm x 65 cm $31\frac{3}{4}''$ x $25\frac{1}{2}''$	60 cm x 81 cm $23\frac{1}{2}''$ x $31\frac{3}{4}''$
#30	92 cm x 73 cm $36''$ x $28\frac{1}{2}''$	65 cm x 92 cm $25\frac{1}{2}''$ x $36''$

CANVAS-STRETCHING PLIERS. Pliers with wide lateral jaws that securely grip the canvas in the stretching process. A small bump on one side is used as a fulcrum in pulling prepared canvas tightly over the edge of the

Canvas-stretching pliers

stretcher strip, in position for tacks or staples. See *Stretching Canvas*.

CAPUT MORTUUM. The obsolete name for a bluish-red earth color made of native iron oxide.

CARDBOARD (Pasteboard). Made by pasting together layers of paper, it is available in different weights and degrees of quality. It is not considered a permanent support for painting, but is the usual backing to which canvas is glued in the manufacture of canvas boards. See also *Illustration Board*.

CARICATURE. The exaggeration and distortion of characteristic physical features of a face or person. Often the term is used only in reference to the portrait. The emphasis on individuality is used both for purely comic effect and, more seriously, for purposes of satire.

CARMINE. A lake color made from a dye taken from a Central American insect. Fades quickly and is no longer used.

CARNAUBA WAX. A hard wax obtained from South American palm leaves. It is used in wax mixtures, making them harder.

CAROLINGIAN. Pertains to the Frankish dynasty beginning with Pepin the Short, in A.D. 750. In the 9th and 10th centuries there was a short-lived renaissance initiated by the Emperor Charlemagne's effort to revive the Classicism of Rome. This was called the Carolingian Renaissance.

CARTOON. A full-scale preparatory drawing on paper for a painting on plaster or canvas. Also, a cartoon can be a humorous or satirical drawing.

CARTOUCHE (kahr-TOOSH). (Fr.) A scroll-like ornament, especially found in Baroque design, and often used as a field for coat-of-arms symbols, etc. Also, an oval or

Cartouche of a German heraldic shield, 16th century.

Cartouches of the Egyptian King Mer-ne-ptah (c. 1200 B.C.).

oblong shape containing an Egyptian sovereign's name in hieroglyphic.

CASEIN. The water-color technique that uses glue as a binder. It differs from gouache in that the paint film is water resistant and, once dry, can no longer be reworked. See also *Glue.*

CASSEL EARTH. See *Vandyke Brown.*

CAST. See *Plaster Cast.*

CAST SHADOW. See *Shadow.*

CAVE PAINTING. See *Prehistoric Painting.*

CENTER OF VISION. See *Linear Perspective.*

CENTIMETER (cm.). A unit of measure, equal to $\frac{1}{100}$ meter. As many publications have reproductions with the dimensions of the original paintings given in the metric system, the equivalents are supplied:

1 centimeter (cm.) = 0.3937 in.   1 inch = 2.54 cm.
1 meter (m.)   = 39.37 in.   1 foot = 0.3048 m.

For an approximate but quick conversion from centimeters to inches, the following formulas can be used:

$$2/5 \text{ x cm.} = \text{inches} \quad or \quad \frac{\text{cm.}}{2.5} = \text{inches}$$

CERULEAN BLUE. The true pigment is an artificially produced, bright, cool opaque blue made from a compound of cobalt and tin oxides. It is a good drier and is permanent. Often, cheaper substitutes consisting of mixtures of French ultramarine or phthalo blue are mislabeled cerulean blue.

CHALK. Artificially prepared calcium carbonate, usually called precipitated chalk. Whiter and purer than native calcium carbonate, it is used with glue binders in water mediums for gesso grounds for oil and tempera.

CHAMOIS SKIN (often pronounced SHAM-ee). A soft piece of leather, made from the skin of a goat, deer, or sheep, that is used as an erasing cloth when drawing with charcoal. Originally made from the skin of the chamois.

CHARCOAL. A carbon black available (a) in thin sticks of different degrees of hardness, (b) ground and compressed in chalklike crayons, (c) in pencil form, and (d) powdered for pouncing. The stick form is made by roasting close-grained woods such as willow or beech. The best quality is charred vine. Charcoal is used by the painter to make easily corrected studies and drawings on paper as well as the preliminary composition directly on the canvas. It has been known since prehistoric times.

CHEF-D'OEUVRE (sheh-DOO-vrih). (Fr.)   A masterpiece. See *Masterpiece*.

CHIAROSCURO (kee-ah-roh-SKEW-ro). (It.)   The use of light and shadow, the general arrangement of the lights and darks in a picture. The term is used to describe the effects of modeling and dark and light (the use of incident light, strong light source, reflected light, cast shadows, etc.) to give the illusion of the existence of volumes in space. See also *Modeling* and *Shadow*.

CHINA CLAY. Native hydrated aluminum silicate. Used chiefly as an adulterant in paints—also in making chinaware.

CHINESE BLUE. See *Prussian Blue.*

CHINESE VERMILION. See *Vermilion.*

CHINESE WHITE. The name given to a water-color white made of zinc oxide. See also *Zinc White.*

CHINOISERIE (shee-nwahz-REE). (Fr.) A term occasionally still used to describe Chinese art, original or imitation, as well as European art inspired by Oriental art.

CHROMA. See *Color.*

CHROMATIC COLOR. See *Color.*

CHROME PIGMENTS. Artificially produced from lead chromates. A variety of hues running through greenish yellows, oranges, and reds. They are poisonous, are not permanent, and have been replaced by the cadmium pigments.

CHROMIUM OXIDE GREEN OPAQUE. A dense, strong, opaque olive green of good covering power. Permanent.

CHROMIUM OXIDE GREEN TRANSPARENT. See *Viridian.*

CINNABAR. An obsolete term for natural vermilion. See *Vermilion.* The term also was onced used in "green cinnabar" to describe a mixture of Prussian blue and chrome yellow.

CINQUECENTO (chin-kway-CHEN-toh). (It.) The 1500's, or 16th century.

CLASSICAL ART. Generally refers to the art, sculptural

42

and architectural, of the Greek nation of the 5th century B.C. and to the related Roman variations. Classical Art is characterized by dignity and reserve, and by an idealized representation of the human form. The term has come to mean all subsequent art that conforms to the models and rules of these antique examples.

CLEANING OF PAINTINGS. The cleaning of oil paintings consists mainly of removing old yellowed varnish with its accumulated dirt, soot, fly specks, etc. Care must be taken not to disturb any delicate glazes or films of color. The usual method is to rub the surface gently with wads of absorbent cotton lightly moistened with turpentine, followed immediately with dry cotton wads. (The painting is laid horizontally and the surface supported from behind.) No aqueous solutions or soaps are used. Any more extensive cleaning with more powerful solvents or with scalpels is best left to experienced restorers.

CLEAVAGE. Cracking of the paint film in which it separates from the ground and flakes off in pieces.

CLOISONNISME (klwah-zoh-NEEZ-mih). (Fr.) A style in French painting that derives its name from *cloisonné* enameling (which is done by filling with enamel areas that have been outlined with metal "fences"). Thus, in painting, the style consists of flat decorative areas of color, strongly outlined. See *Synthetism.*

CLOSED COMPOSITION. A constructed equilibrium obtained by keeping the directional movements within the limits of the picture's edges, making the composition a self-contained entity, with an allover feeling of intention and planned design. Closed compositions are said to have a tectonic, or architectural, quality. See also *Composition* and *Tectonic.*

CLOSED EXHIBITION. See *Exhibition.*

CLOSED FORM. A mass completely enclosed and separated from surrounding space. The term also pertains to closed composition. See also *Closed Composition* and *Form.*

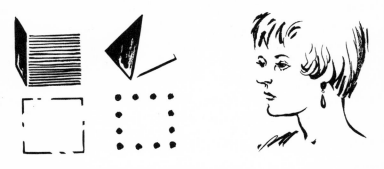

Several examples of closure.

CLOSURE. A term used to describe the perceptual completion on the part of a viewer of an area, a shape, etc., which has not been completely presented in actuality. See also *Gestalt,* 2.

CLOVES, OIL OF. Once used to disguise objectionable smells, and also as a drying retarder. See *Retarder.*

COACH VARNISH. A cooked oil-copal varnish originally used on English coaches. When well made it was pale and very hard, but still had a tendency to yellow. See also *Varnish.*

COAL-TAR PIGMENTS. See *Aniline Colors.*

COBALT BLUE. The true pigment, also called Thénard's blue, is made from compounds of cobalt oxide. It is a bright clear blue, more greenish than ultramarine, and somewhat similar to cerulean blue. It is a good drier and is permanent. Often, cheaper substitutes consisting of mixtures of French ultramarine or phthalo blue are mislabeled cobalt blue.

COBALT DRIER (Cobalt Linoleate Drier). See *Drier*.

COBALT VIOLET. A pigment artificially produced from different sources: cobalt arsenite, which is poisonous and to be avoided, and cobalt phosphate. Made in a range of shades from deep blue-violet to a lighter reddish-violet, both pigments are good driers and are permanent.

COBALT YELLOW (Aureolin). Cobalt-potassium nitrate. It is a bright transparent color replacing gamboge.

COLD-PRESSED LINSEED OIL. See *Linseed Oil*.

COLLAGE (koh-LAHZH). (Fr.) The process, or a picture itself, made up of scraps of paper, cloth, string, wood veneer, etc., pasted (*collé*) to the surface of the canvas. There may or may not be additional drawing or painting involved. *Papiers collés* (pasted papers) use bits of newspapers, wallpapers, playing and visiting cards, ticket stubs, cigar bands, etc.

COLLÉ (koh-LAY). (Fr.) Pasted. See *Collage*.

COLLECTOR. See *Patron*.

COLOGNE EARTH. See *Vandyke Brown*.

COLOR. Color exists through light. Light is electromagnetic energy of visible wave lengths on the radiant spectrum, where it appears between the infrared or heat rays and the ultraviolet rays. Light that is composed of the rays of all of the visible wave lengths is white. This white light, projected through a prism, can be separated by refraction into the different wave lengths. These rays, when they stimulate the receptors in the retina of the eye, become color sensations. They are the prismatic colors of the visible spectrum, and range from red, through orange, yellow, yellow-green, green, blue-green, blue, blue-violet, to violet. Naturally, the source of the light will govern the composition of its rays and therefore its color.

The painter is interested in the behavior of light as it operates to produce color in the visible world—on objects, surfaces, and through atmosphere, etc. Light is reflected, transmitted, and/or absorbed by objects. The white light of sun projected through stained glass, for example, becomes filtered light, and the color of the glass may register as film color. If this color looks red, then all the wave lengths, except those of red, have been absorbed. Looking through a tender leaf held to the sun, we also see filtered light—in this case, green. The same leaf held away from

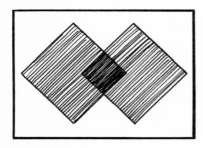

Subtractive or
paint color mixing.

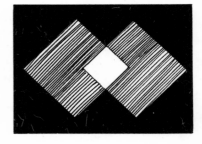

Additive or
light color mixing

the source of light will show reflected light and the leaf will have a green surface color. A glass of sauterne will give a three-dimensional volume color of pale yellow.

Although color exists through light, and a knowledge of light is important to the painter, he works with paint. Paint is made of different pigments, which vary in molecu-

46

lar structure. These variations and differences produce in each pigment its characteristic ability to absorb, transmit, or reflect particular wave lengths of light. This ability, under regulated conditions, gives them their respective color effects. As procedures, the mixing of paint and the mixing of light are related but complementary. The colors of light change by the additive process in mixing. With paint, each color mixed absorbs or subtracts from the total rays reflected; thus, the mixing process is subtractive.

Color may be classified as chromatic—showing a definite hue, or achromatic—without hue, as in neutral grays between black and white. Color has qualities that give it its differentiation. The most important of these are:

Hue. This relates to a color's position in the spectrum, based on its wave length. Basically, hue is its characteristic "color," as red, orange, green, blue, violet, etc. (A brown could be an impure red hue; an ocher, an impure yellow, etc.)

Intensity. A color's saturation, also called its chroma. This is also its purity. The more intense the color, the less diluted by black, white, gray, or a complementary color. It can be measured by the extent to which it departs from a neutral gray of the same value. A color lightened by white is called a tint, while a color darkened by black is called a shade.

Subjective associative qualities. For instance:
Red—excitement, life, blood, heat.
Yellow—happiness, sunshine, gold.
Green—restfulness, vegetation, coolness.
Blue—calmness, lightness, the heavens, cold.

Temperature. A relative term based somewhat on psychological sensation. Reds and oranges are considered "warm" colors, and blues and greens "cool." A bluish-red would be "cooler" than a pure red, and a yellow-green "warmer" than a blue-green. Temperature also affects a color's seeming distance or depth, as warmer colors appear to advance or be closer, and cooler colors appear to recede or be at greater depth in space.

Value. The lightness or darkness of a color measured against the scale of white to black. Value is also used as a comparison. For example, a pure yellow hue is of lighter value than a pure blue; however, if the blue were lightened with an addition of white (changing its intensity and hue, of course), it would approach the yellow in value.

In conclusion, one could say that the painter sees *color as light,* thinks of *color as paint,* works with *color as pigment,* transposing it through *color as sensation* into *color as expression.* See also *Color Wheel.*

COLOR CHORD. See *Color Wheel.*

COLOR FATIGUE. See *Afterimage.*

COLOR FIELD PAINTING. A relative term used to describe painting that gains its effect from more or less flat biomorphic areas of color that have been spontaneously applied. The canvas is sometimes painted in a horizontal position with the liquid paint being flooded onto the surface.

COLOR MODULATION. See *Color* and *Modulation.*

COLOR SCATTERING. The term refers to the propensity of the atmosphere to scatter light of the shorter wave lengths (at the blue end of the spectrum) more than light of the longer wave lengths (at the red end of the spectrum). This gives the sky its characteristic blue color, and is a factor in aerial perspective. See also *Aerial Perspective* and *Color.*

COLOR STUDY AND THEORY. Man has always been intrigued by color, and the close relationship of light and color has been studied since the Greek civilization. Certain men have made definite contributions to the knowledge of the phenomena of vision—a process that is still not completely understood. A partial listing of distinguished names associated with an intellectual or scientific contribution to the study of color would include:

Leonardo da Vinci (1452–1519). Recorded many acute observations on optics, light and shadow, and aerial perspective. He recognized the colors of the rainbow (the spectrum of sunlight) and their appearance in Nature.

I. Newton (1642–1727). English physicist and philosopher who, with the use of the prism, broke up white light into the colors of the spectrum and recombined them. He was the first to develop a color wheel.

J. W. von Goethe (1749–1832). German writer and scientist who, as early as 1810, disagreed with Newton's theories of light. He recognized afterimages and their relation to light primaries and complementaries.

T. Young (1773–1829). English physicist, physician, and linguist who explored the physiological aspects of vision, and whose optical theories were later developed by Helmholtz.

M. E. Chevreul (1786–1889). French chemist who, in 1839, published his theories on the principles and laws of color harmony and contrast. He had a great influence on French painting, from Delacroix through the Neo-Impressionists.

H. von Helmholtz (1821–1894). German physicist, biologist, and physician, who extended Young's theories of color and vision, and was also a pioneer in the field of physiological optics. The Young-Helmholtz theory of color vision, as it is now known, was presented in 1867.

J. C. Maxwell (1831–1879). Scottish physicist who developed the rotating discs to study the optical mixtures of color.

O. N. Rood (1831–1902). American professor of physics

who, in 1879, published a book for artists that included calculations on the luminosity of optical mixtures and values of light. He had considerable influence on Munsell. **W. Ostwald** (1853–1932). German physio-chemist who developed a three-dimensional color system based on a twenty-four hued circle with tints and shades. See *Color Systems*.

A. H. Munsell (1859–1918). American artist who developed around 1913 an extensive color system, based on the five- and ten-hued color circle with tints and shades at progressive intervals. His is the most complete and widely used color index to date.

See *Color Systems*.

COLOR SYSTEMS. For purposes of color identification and uniformity in matching colors, etc., various color systems of notation have been developed. These are important to industry. Few painters make extensive use of them except as an additional means of exploring the relationships and possibilities of color. The two most accepted systems are the Ostwald Color System, and the Munsell Color System, both three-dimensional in form. The Ostwald Color System is based on twenty-four hues around the equator of a color "solid." The intensity is greatest at the surface or outer edge and decreases as it approaches the axis. The value is lightest at the top and darkest at the bottom. The Munsell Color System consists of five principal hues plus five intermediate hues. These are placed in a color circle at a position of "five," in the third-dimensional range of values of "ten," running from white at the top to black at the bottom. Intensity or chroma increases as it goes out from the neutral axis. The steps or intervals in this system are based on a judgment of the eye rather than any photometric measurement. See also *Color*.

COLOR TEMPERATURE. See *Color*.

COLOR WHEEL. Taking the visible spectrum, the painter bends it around in a diagrammatic circle, joining the violet end to the red. This gives him a practical chart of color relationships of both the primary (purest and most intense) hues of light (red, green, and blue-violet), and of the primary hues of paint (yellow, cyan blue, and magenta red). Using the primary hues of paint, the artist can obtain—theoretically, at least—all the other hues.

Although this simplified chart is arbitrary, many basic relationships can be visualized. For example, it shows that the light primaries lie opposite the paint primaries, and are therefore their complementaries. True paint comple-

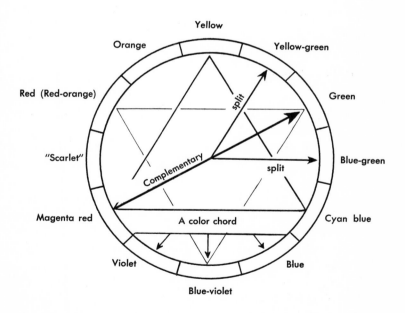

A typical 12-hued color wheel.

51

mentaries, when mixed in proper proportions, produce an achromatic color—a neutral gray. The color wheel can show the two hues used to make a "split complementary," those on each side of the complementary. Analogous colors, or those containing a common hue, sometimes called a color chord, are readily apparent—as well as their common complementary. Also, for purposes of mixing, it can be seen that, when two paint primaries are combined, they produce a secondary hue that is, as well, a light primary. The intermediary hues between the secondaries are sometimes called the tertiary hues.

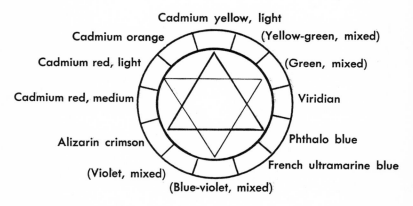

A simple oil medium 12-hued
color wheel, using eight pigments

Pigments, the actual materials that make paint, do not necessarily correspond to the true hues on the color wheel. Yet, a simple and practical chart for a limited number of oil pigments can be made as an approximation. See also *Color.*

COLOUR. An alternate spelling of "color." See *Color.*

COMBINE. See *Found Object.*

COMPLEMENTARY COLORS. See *Color* and *Color Wheel.*

COMPOSITION. The organization of all the pictorial components of a drawing or painting and the creation of a plastic entity. The process of designing. Also the name given to the result. See also *Design* and *Plastic.*

CONCEPTUAL PAINTING. The emphasis in this approach in painting is on the arrangement of images according to a prepared or set conception in the mind of the artist, rather than on what he perceives at the moment and directly with his eyes. This contrasts with the more immediate perceptual approach.

CONCOURS. See *Hors Concours.*

CONE OF VISION. See *Linear Perspective.*

CONSERVATION OF PAINTINGS. This term encompasses the complex field of the analysis of damage, rehabilitation, and preservation of paintings. See *Relining* and *Restoration.*

CONSTRUCTIVISM. A development around 1917 of Cubism and Futurism in Russia. Later, as a reaction to the disruption of World War I, it involved itself in engineering and architecture and made use of a variety of materials in geometrical and mathematical forms. The movement was suppressed by the new regime in Russia, but many of its artists emigrated to other parts of Europe and to America, spreading its philosophy.

CONTÉ. A trade name for colored square-shaped chalk crayons. They are black, white, brownish red, and bistre, and all are in different degrees of hardness.

CONTEMPORARY. The literal meaning of the word is "living, occurring, or existing at the same period of time," and it has come to be used in art criticism when referring to painting produced by living artists or to the artists themselves.

CONTENT. The meaning of a painting—its *raison d'être,* or aesthetic justification.

Top view, showing lines of sight tangent to the turn of the form.

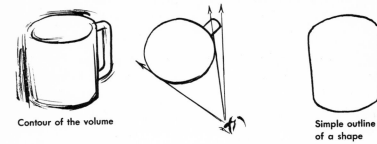

Contour of the volume

Simple outline
of a shape

CONTOUR. The bounding line of a volume of three-dimensional form, observed where it follows the turn of the form at the limit of its projection into space. As a line, it may be lost in darkness or in bright light, may be part of space or of another form, or may be blurred or veiled.

Examples of contrapposto. (FROM MICHELANGELO)

CONTRAPPOSTO. (It.) A term used to describe the

opposing twist between masses. Usually this is in a figure, and is the difference between the direction of the shoulders and the direction of the hips. In some Italian painting of the 16th century, this became considerably exaggerated.

CONTRAPUNTAL. A term borrowed from music and used in art criticism. It refers to the combining of melodies according to the laws of counterpoint. In painting, it is the simultaneous presentation of two (or more) themes or ideas, which together make up a meaningful and artistic expression, and the relationship of the abstract elements of line and shape, for instance, separated yet working together.

CONTRAST. Contrast is one of the important basic factors in art; we see only because of its existence. In painting, it is created by the differences in elements of design as they appear in the same composition. Contrasts nearly always are found in combinations. The main contrasts are:

Area. Differences in size, area, or amount.
Color or hue. Complementary hues offer the greatest contrast. Warm to cool contrasts change the hue and can indicate depth. Hue contrast gives a great range even without value or intensity differences.
Detail. Depicted detail contrasted with open or simplified areas.
Intensity. Purity of color contrasted with grayed color or mixed tones.
Movement. Related to directional and linear contrast.
Shape. Related to area and edge contrast.
Texture. Differences in the surface effect of either the actual paint and support, or of the objects depicted.
Value. The basic dark and light differences, also called tonal differences.

Generally speaking, the more the contrast, the more alive and strong the feeling; the less the contrast, the more quiet and gentle. An important factor in the evaluation of contrast is the human tendency to increase or accentuate the contrast while evaluating it. See also *Simultaneous Contrast*.

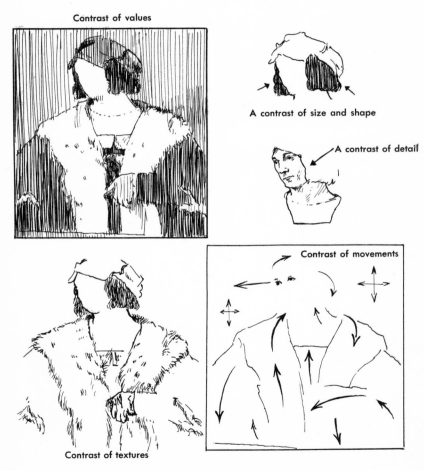

Examples of different contrasts. (FROM TITIAN)

COOKED OIL-RESIN VARNISH. See *Varnish.*

COOL COLOR. See *Color.*

COPAIBA BALSAM. Also spelled "copaiva." See *Oleoresin.*

COPAL. See *Resin* and *Varnish.*

COPY. Modern copies or imitations of paintings of the "Old Masters" by students or copyists are easily recognized and are never intended to deceive; however, copies of contemporary artists' works are sometimes intended to be accepted as originals and as such are forgeries. Some artists make copies of their own paintings. These may be identical (replicas), or they may be made with slight variations. In both cases they are considered to be legitimate works.

COTTON. A fabric used for a painting support. See *Canvas.*

C.P. Abbreviation for the term "Chemically Pure"; used to indicate a grade of material as free as possible from impurities or extenders.

CRACKS IN PAINTING. Cracks can be of several different patterns, but nearly all are due to the movement (contraction and expansion) of the ground, paint, and varnish layers relative to one another. The characteristic

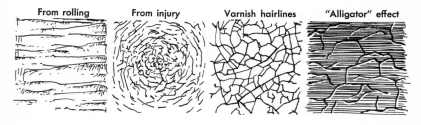

Examples of cracks in painting.

cracks of a "lizard skin" or "alligator" effect result from extreme movement such as may come from painting a quick-drying layer of paint over one still wet, or a brittle layer over one more flexible. In many 19th-century paintings, cracks were due to the use of bitumen. Extreme changes of temperature or humidity, in addition to the obvious maltreatment of a painting by rolling it up, can produce cracks. See *Craquelure*.

CRADLING. A term used in the conservation of paintings to describe the application of criss-crossed strips glued to the back of wood panels to prevent them from warping and buckling. It is a somewhat complicated process as allowance must be made for movement (contraction and expansion) due to moisture. This occurs in one direction only, across the grain. The term has also come to be applied to the strengthening of wallboard panels by the gluing of a bracing frame to the back.

CRAFTSMANSHIP. The basic excellence of skill in the mechanics of painting. A concern for the manual or technical factors in the process of producing a painting, as separate from the aesthetic considerations.

CRAQUELURE (krah-keh-LYOOR). (Fr.) The pattern of hair-line cracks commonly found on old paintings, and occasionally on recent ones painted with faulty techniques. The absence of true *craquelure* on an old painting may sometimes indicate a forgery. See *Cracks in Painting*.

CRAWLING. A flexible paint or varnish layer when placed over a hard, glossy, nonabsorbent one will crack, and the edges recede, resulting in open fissures. This is called crawling.

CREATIVE. Having the ability to create. To create is "to bring into being, to cause to exist, to produce a work of imagination" (Webster).

CRECHE (kraysh). (Fr.) A crib or manger; more familiarly, that of the infant Jesus, in the stable at Bethlehem, encircled by Mary, Joseph, the shepherds, the Magi, and the sheep and cattle.

CREMNITZ WHITE. See *Flake White.*

CRETAN PAINTING. See *Minoan Painting.*

CRIMSON. A bluish-red close to the primary paint hue of red; a magenta red.

CRISP PAINT. See *Short Paint.*

CRITIC. The professional art critic is primarily a writer, using words to assess, interpret, and explain the painter's work to the public. The ideal critic is sensitive and sincere, and has the important quality of discrimination. He has a well-rounded education in the history of art, combined with the active knowledge of the mechanisms and perplexities of painting. His profession encompasses elements characteristic of the scholar, the art historian, and the philosopher. Although he is acquainted with painters and their efforts, he retains an allover objectivity when considering individuals, styles, and movements.

CROQUIS (kro-KEE). (Fr.) A rough sketch, or sometimes a sketching group or class.

CROSSHATCHING. See *Hatching.*

CUBISM. A remarkable evolution of 20th-century painting growing out of the efforts of Picasso (1881–   ) and Braque (1882–1963), in attempting to solve the plastic problems involved in the relationship of two-dimensional space to the illusion of three-dimensional form. In part, this concern with structural qualities was directly traceable to the innovations of Cézanne. In 1906–1908, Picasso was under the influences of Negro sculpture, and Braque, in 1907, was strongly influenced by Cézanne. Working

59

jointly, they produced the first forms of "faceted" Cubism (1908–1909) in which objects were broken into small facets or planes. By 1909 this first stage of Cubism established it as a distinct and valid art form, since called Analytical Cubism. This development reached its high point about 1912, and was concerned with the analysis of form and volume to the exclusion of color, restricting the latter to shades of black, white, and ochers. Form was decomposed, simplified to geometric shape, and reassembled from multiple points of view in an abstractly organized space. *Papiers Collés,* or pasted paper—newsprint, wallpaper, calling cards, etc.—and other materials such as imitation wood grain were added to the canvas surface as textural areas to accent the physical reality of the painting. Synthetic Cubism was the name given to the final stage of Cubism, from 1913 to 1914. In this period, color was re-employed in addition to a more spontaneous or arbitrary building up of objects through flat shapes. The strong color used in textural patterns was reminiscent of the earlier use of *collage.* Cubism led into such movements as Constructivism, Futurism, and Orphism.

CUTTLEBONE. The calcified shell of the cuttlefish sometimes used as an abrasive to remove glossy paint films and give a tooth to the surface.

CYANINE BLUE. In most pigments, it is a mixture of cobalt and Prussian blue. In four-color or "full-color process" printing (with yellow, red, blue, and black) and in color photography, the blue (a greenish-turquoise) is called *cyan.* In that case, it is usually made of an aniline dye. As a paint hue, it can be considered the primary blue hue. See also *Color Wheel.*

D

DADA. An antirational and antiaesthetic movement founded in Zurich in 1916. It was in part motivated by a disillusionment with society and disgust with and protest against World War I. It anticipated Surrealism in its desire to outrage, shock, and generally exasperate; yet, from its perversity came many significant works of art. According to one of its most eloquent spokesmen, Duchamp (1887–), "Dada was . . . a way to avoid being influenced by one's immediate environment, or by the past. . . ." See *Surrealism.*

DAMMAR. Also spelled "damar." See *Resin* and *Varnish.*

DARK AND LIGHT. (Also Light and Dark.) A term used to describe the disposition and changes of value relative to the range of grays between black and white—with color translated as value. The distribution of the darks and lights in a painting develops from illumination plus the values of the local colors. See also *Chiaroscuro* and *Value.*

DEALER. The dealer in paintings of contemporary artists acts as their agent or representative. His primary responsibility to the artist is in exhibition and sales, and he handles promotion, accounting, and other routine but necessary activities. Many dealers are more than business associates, and have become confidential friends and advisers to their artist. They have often subsidized individual painters because of faith in their eventual recognition. The average dealer represents approximately fifteen to twenty artists, and manages a gallery to exhibit their work. He takes it on consignment, selling it at a commission of usually 33⅓ per cent. He furnishes space for a one-man show of about three weeks, usually once a year. Some dealers buy the painter's work outright with the expectancy of later selling it at a profit. Dealers are increasingly recognizing their responsibilities to the public, as well as to the artist, a development exemplified in the formation of associations such as the Art Dealers Association of America. See also *Gallery*.

DECORATION. One of the purposes for which paintings have long been produced (and continue to be) is decoration—the giving of pleasure by the embellishment of an environment. Pure decoration, not essential to the function of that which it decorates, is considered ornament, without content or meaning. To evaluate any decoration, one must become involved with aspects of the justification of art. See also *Embellishment* and *Ornament*.

DEEP. See *Light-Medium-Deep*.

DÉJÀ VU (day-zhah VIU). (Fr.) The term refers to something "already seen," or that which has been seen before.

DÉMODÉ (day-moh-DAY). (Fr.) Old-fashioned, out of style.

DEPTH. A term used in referring to the evaluation of distance perpendicular to the picture plane and into the three-dimensional space of the picture box. Thus, a painting can have height and width (of the picture plane) and (illusional) depth. See also *Picture Box*.

DERNIER CRI, Le (luh dair-nyay KREE). (Fr.) The latest thing (cry), or the newest fashion.

DESIGN. The framework or constructive scaffold of a composition or a finished work of art. The disposition of the pictorial elements of shape, form, line, space, light, etc., and the organization of the co-ordinating principles of harmony, balance, rhythm, proportion, unity, variety, etc. See also *Composition*.

62

DETAIL. The delineation of relatively small elements, shapes, and patterns, or a particularization that holds the viewer's interest in contrast to more empty areas of the painting. Also, in printed reproductions, the term means a section or a fragment of an entire painting.

DEXTRIN. See *Glue.*

DIFFUSE REFLECTION. See *Reflection, Light.*

DIFFUSION. The spreading out of light in the process of reflection from a surface or in the transmission through the atmosphere. This may blur edges and blend areas, shapes, and colors, as in aerial perspective. See also *Reflection, Light.*

DILETTANTE. (It.) One who loves art but practices it only for amusement and in a superficial way. See also *Amateur.*

DILUENT. A diluting or dissolving agent, which thins and increases fluidity. See *Thinner.*

DIPTYCH (DIP-tik). (Gr.) A painting in two parts.

DIRECTION. In painting, visual direction is the line or course upon which a pictorial element is projected to move; it is also the line on which any visual force moves. Directional force is created by such factors as:

Attraction. Resulting from the location of related weights, and the tensions between objects of mass and volume.

The axes of shapes and volumes. As these axes approximate the vertical or the horizontal, a directional pull is created.

Distortion. Such as elongation.

Gravity. The strong downward pull has a psychological effect on the relationship of the upper to the lower areas of the picture, and sets the optical center.

Interval. A change in interval creates a strong directional force.

Subject matter. As in the action of the pointing finger, the turned profile, the glancing eyes, or the walking figure. See also *Movement*.

DISSONANCE. A term taken from music and pertaining to a relationship of simultaneously existing elements in a degree of discord. Dissonance is unresolved, incomplete, and restless. It is created by variable tensions between such elements as colors and shapes, and the factors of weight and movement. Unlike contrast, dissonance is always unsatisfying.

DISTEMPER. Water-color paint with a glue-size binder. The term has been used to distinguish the gouache-like mixtures, which may be redissolved after they have dried, from the emulsions of true tempera, which, in dried films, are highly water resistant.

DISTORTION. In painting, distortion is the manipulation and changing of values, forces, shapes, proportions,

Examples of distortion. (LEFT FROM EL GRECO—*detail,* RIGHT FROM CÉZANNE—detail)

etc. Achieved by exaggeration, diminution, and general modification of the norm, the usual, or the expected, distortion is a basic means of achieving tensions and thereby heightened expression and communication. It does not, in itself, denote any inartistic or negative quality.

DIVISIONISM. See *Neo-Impressionism.*

DOMINANCE. One of the interrelating principles of design. Dominance designates the most powerful or conspicuous of a combination of elements. It also is found in the climax of a series, or in the repetition of a single element. It can be manifested in the center of interest or in the most significant area of the composition, and is closely related to unity. See also *Unity.*

DOUBLE IMAGERY. The use of a pictorial representation that can be seen or interpreted in two different ways. For instance, a detailed landscape might be also a profile; a nest with three eggs might be also a face with eyes and nose. Some examples are obvious and are common in fantastic art; others are more subtle and involve symbolic meanings. See also *Metaphor.*

DRAFTSMANSHIP. (Also known as *draughtsmanship.*) The ability to draw. Although mechanical drawing is referred to as drafting, the term "draftsmanship" refers to drawing of all kinds. See *Drawing.*

DRAUGHTSMANSHIP. See *Draftsmanship.*

DRAWING. The delineation or the portrayal by use of line and/or tone of an idea or object. And the result of such delineation. There are two basically different types of drawing: artistic and mechanical. (1) Artistic drawing includes free-hand drawing, preliminary sketches and studies—and any linear or tonal pictorial representation that is the result of a highly creative act. It involves an understanding obtained by experiencing, through all of the artist's senses, both appearance and reality. (2) Mechanical drawing (drafting) includes architectural, engineering, and precision drawing; in all of these, considerable use is made of mechanical aids such as T-squares, triangles, rulers, and compasses.

DRIER. A material (a *siccative*) that hastens the drying rate of paint mixed with it. It acts as a catalyst, accelerating the oxidation. Excessive use of driers can cause cracking and discoloration. The safest or least harmful of the siccatives is the cobalt linoleate drier; not to be recommended is the *Siccatif de Courtrai,* or *Siccatif de Haarlem.* Driers are often added to paint in its manufacture. The term is also used when referring to a pigment that dries comparatively quickly.

DRYING OIL. A vegetable oil that dries to form a tough, flexible, adhesive film. The drying is not by evaporation, as it is the case with volatile thinners, but by oxidation and chemical change. The drying oils, acting as binders, are combined (ground) with dry pigment to form paint. They are also used in painting mediums in the process of applying the paint to its support. The usual drying oil is linseed oil in various forms: cold-pressed, refined, sun-thickened, and stand oil. Other drying oils include poppyseed oil, walnut oil, and safflower oil. See also *Linseed Oil.*

DRYING RATE. The comparative speed with which the various oil pigments dry. This ranges from that of the rapid driers, such as flake white and the umbers, to the very slow driers—ivory black and the cadmiums. Manufacturers sometimes add small amounts of driers to the slow-drying paints, and slow-drying oils to the fast-drying paints, to compensate for the differences.

DRY PIGMENT. The powdered form of a material

66

which, when ground in a suitable liquid vehicle, makes paint. The dry pigment itself is the same in various techniques of painting, i.e., oil, tempera, water color, etc., even though the vehicle or medium may differ.

DUCO. The trade name for a lacquer. See *Lacquer.*

DUTCH WHITE. White lead pigment made by the old Dutch process. Also can be the name given to China clay, or native hydrated aluminum silicate, used as an adulterant or to make chinaware.

DYE. See *Pigments.*

DYNAMIC. Pertains to energy and vitality. Describes any element of a painting that is in movement and that is an active and influential force. The opposite of static.

E

EARTH COLORS. A name given to the pigments mined from the earth, and used either in their native state or roasted. They derive their color from iron compounds: oxides, hydroxides, and silicates, and also manganese. They consist of the true ochers, siennas, umbers, and green-earth, raw and burnt. Sometimes included in the "earth colors" are those pigments artificially produced to replace certain red earths: Indian red, light red, and Venetian red.

EASEL. The stand that holds the painting as the artist works. The heavy studio easel, on casters, is adjustable for height (generally by ratchet or screw) and angle of tilt. The sketching easel is a light, collapsible, and portable

Studio and sketching easels.

tripod. There are also decorative easels for display purposes.

EASEL PAINTING. A term used to distinguish a painting from a mural. A painting is on canvas or panel, which is portable, and never permanently glued to the wall. The mural, however, may be painted on canvas, while held on an easel, and later affixed to the wall.

ECLECTICISM. In painting the term refers to the practice of the artist in selecting and combining in his own work elements, forms, or concepts of his predecessors. Although there is a natural tradition of influence, eclecticism becomes apparent when the derivations are unassimilated or mutually incompatible. Precisely, the term "Eclectic" has been applied to the Carracci, related Bolognese academic painters of the later half of the 16th century.

ÉCOLE DE PARIS, L' (lay-KOHL duh pah-REE). (Fr.) The School of Paris. See *Paris, School of*.

ÉCOLE DES BEAUX-ARTS, L' (lay-KOHL day boh-ZAHR). (Fr.) The official School of Fine Arts in Paris, founded in 1648, which subscribes to the traditional views of the French Academy.

ÉCORCHÉ (ay-kor-SHAY). (Fr.) A name given to the flayed anatomical figure, usually made of plaster, used in the study of the muscles. Also an illustration of same.

ECRU. No exact color, but a so-called beige or the warm yellowish-gray of unbleached cloth, after which the color was named.

Écorché.

EDGE. The actual limits of an area, two-dimensional shape, or plane. It can have qualities of attraction, texture, movements, etc. See also *Contour*.

EFFLORESCENCE. The property of drying out and powdering due to the loss of the water of crystallization.

EGG YOKE. See *Tempera*.

EGYPTIAN BLUE. An ancient pigment made from copper silicates. Replaced by cobalt blue. Also any number of cool turquoise blues.

EGYPTIAN PAINTING. The history of Ancient Egypt

has been divided into three main kingdoms or empires, with a total of thirty dynasties. Early Egypt and the Old Kingdom (or Old Empire) has been dated as beginning anywhere from c. 4500 B.C. to c. 3100 B.C. and extending to 2475 B.C. or 2200 B.C. The Middle Kingdom (or Middle Empire) is dated 2050 B.C. to 1800 B.C.; and the New Kingdom (or New Empire) from 1570 B.C. to 1090 B.C. Ten of the thirty dynasties existed between 1090 B.C. and the conquest of Alexander the Great in 332 B.C. The earliest examples of Egyptian painting are to be found on the painted pottery taken from prehistoric tombs. These have a relationship to the cave paintings of Paleolithic Europe. Later, paintings are to be found as murals on the walls of the tombs of ancient chieftains and kings. Even in prehistoric times, these showed a racial unity evolving from earlier African and Asiatic elements and influences. Around 3100 B.C., a painting style began its development, and subsequently retained its character for the entire history of Egypt up to the influence of Roman art. This style was based on a conceptual idea of the visible world, strongly illustrative, yet with a feeling for design and use of two-dimensional space in a decorative way. The forms were depicted essentially in line with flat color. There was no attempt at shading or perspective. The human figure was always represented as follows: head in profile; eye and shoulders, front view; hips, legs, and feet, profile. The subject matter of the murals was of great variety. There were those of religious nature, such as kings making offerings to gods; there were records of wars and hunts; and, as could be expected from a food-producing economy, there were scenes of everyday life—the cultivation of grain, the raising of livestock, the making of boats, furniture, jewelry, etc. All of these varied activities had a utilitarian purpose, that of providing the dead with both the necessities and the pleasures of life. These murals were generally painted over reliefs carved into the stone walls of the tombs. Later it was common, when the surface was too uneven, to lay over the stone a thin coat of stucco or plaster. True fresco was not used however, the paint being applied with some sort of gum-binding medium. Egypt had a very active civilization down to approximately 1000 b.c., as evidenced by clay-floor paintings and illustrations on papyrus as well as tomb murals. About the second century a.d., it became a custom to adorn mummies with a portrait head. This was painted either on linen cloth or on a panel of wood with wax and resin colors, and was rendered in a more realistic Western style.

EIGHT, The. See *Ashcan School.*

ÉLAN VITAL (ay-lahn vee-TAHL). (Fr.) The vital force; one's inner dynamic creativity.

EMBELLISHMENT. An enhancement of a painting by enriching the canvas surface with detailed color nuances, textural variety, and general paint manipulation. This embellishment can function as a valid component of the painting. See also *Paint Quality.*

EMERALD GREEN. Artificially produced from very poisonous compounds of copper and arsenic, it is a very brilliant, but impermanent, pigment. It is also called vert Paul Véronèse, Schweinfurt green, English green, and Paris green; however, it should not be confused with vert émeraude (viridian).

EMOTION. Feeling. See *Feeling.*

EMPATHY. See *Gesture.*

EMPHASIS. A principle of design associated with dominance. See *Dominance.*

EMULSION. A liquid mixture of water with an oily ingredient, held together by an emulsifying element. The egg yolk is a natural emulsion and is used in tempera painting either with the addition of water or with many combinations of oil, water, varnish, gum, etc. See also *Tempera*.

ENAMEL. In painting, the term refers to a paint which dries very hard with a high gloss similar to that of porcelain or a true enamel finish.

ENCAUSTIC PAINTING. Painting with a hot wax medium. The paints, the palette, and, to a certain extent, the support are kept warm in the process. Various manipulations are used, with different brushes and knives, as well as a final allover heating to fuse and help bind the painting together. The support is usually a gesso ground panel. Developed by the ancient Greeks, encaustic painting gradually was displaced by oil and tempera techniques. Recently, however, a renewed interest has been taken in this technique for easel pictures.

EN FACE (ahn FAHS). (Fr.) In front of, facing, or opposite.

ENGAGÉ (ahn-gah-ZHAY). (Fr.) Engaged, involved; the term is used in referring to concerned artists who actively enlist in social and political causes.

ENGLISH GREEN. See *Emerald Green*.

ENGLISH RED. See *Light Red*.

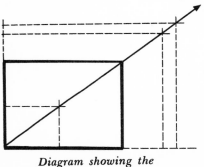

ENLARGEMENT DIAGONAL. The name given to the diagonal used in the process of enlarging (or reducing) a rectangle. Any additional rectangle will retain the same proportions as the original if it is drawn on the same diagonal.

Diagram showing the enlargement diagonal.

72

EN PLEIN AIR (ahn pleh-NAIR). (Fr.) In the open air; generally refers to the Impressionists' method of painting outside, rather than in the studio, and their attempt to capture the quality of the open air in their work.

EN RAPPORT (ahn rah-POHR). (Fr.) In close relationship.

ENSEMBLE (ahn-SAHn-blih). (Fr.) The whole; all the parts taken together.

ÉPATER LE BOURGEOIS (ay-pah-TAY luh boor-ZHWAH). (Fr.) To stun, shock, or amaze the middle class or the average person.

ESSENCE, L'. See *Peinture à L'Essence.*

ESSENTIAL OIL. Any one of a number of odorous extracts (essences) from flowers, fruits, vegetables, spices, etc., once used as diluents and drying retarders in paints. See *Retarder.*

ESTHETICS. An alternate spelling of "aesthetics." See *Aesthetics.*

ETHYL ALCOHOL. See *Alcohol.*

EXHIBITION. Also called a *show.* The showing to the public of an artist's work, generally in the gallery of a dealer or in a museum gallery. Exhibitions are of various types:

Closed exhibition. Has a restriction, usually of organizational affiliation, on who may submit work.
Group exhibition. The work of several artists.
Invitational exhibition. The work of only invited artists, who are usually of established reputation.
Juried exhibition. Has a jury, or panel of judges, that decides on who among the submitting artists will be accepted or rejected. Sometimes the jury will consist of a single person.

One-man exhibition. The work of a single artist.

Open exhibition. Without any restrictions as to nationality, residence, sex, age, or organizational affiliation.

Regional exhibition. Has the restriction of geographical residence. In other words, the submitting artist must live in a certain region or area, e.g., the New England States, or San Diego County.

EXPRESSION. A statement, a communication, a bringing to light of that which is hidden. In a painting, this is the translation of an experience into an image, which carries the meaning and is the content of the painting. The "impression" life makes on a painter becomes, through his efforts to understand it, his "expression."

EXPRESSIONISM. A stylistic development, particularly in Germany, of the early 1900's. It evolved from the aspect of Post-Impressionism that was concerned with emotional identification in the expression of a feeling, often negative or unhappy. This reaction of the artist to life was expressed with tensions, distortions, and contrasts in form, space, and color. Brushwork was usually turbulent and instinctive, and reflected an emphasis on the subjective. Van Gogh is considered to be the spiritual father of Expressionism, together with Ensor and Munch. Representative artists would include Beckmann, Nolde, Kokoschka, Rouault, and Soutine.

EXTEMPORE (eks-TEHM-poh-reh). (L.) A word describing the spontaneous painting of a canvas without sketches or previous studies.

EXTENDER. An inert material (usually white), also called a filler, which is added to a paint to impart qualities not normally inherent in the pigment. These could be bulk or body, brushing properties, improvements in

74

film quality, stability, etc. Alumina hydrate is the most widely used material for extending transparent pigments, and blanc fixe for the heavy. Extenders are also sometimes added as adulterants, which merely cheapen the paint.

EYE LEVEL. See *Linear Perspective*.

EYE PULL. A term that has been given to the attention-drawing characteristic of any object, shape, or color, etc. See also *Weight*.

F

FACETED CUBISM. See *Cubism*.

FACSIMILE. Literally, a copy made exactly the same as the original. In the photo-mechanical copying of drawings especially, the term indicates the reproducing of as many of the qualities of the original as possible.

FAKE. Technically, a fake is a painting (or other work of art) that has been fraudulently changed or added to in order to increase its value. It has come to mean a forgery. See also *Forgery*.

FANTASTIC ART. Found in the art of all periods, it is characterized by the imaginative, and the enigmatic. Bosch (c. 1450–1516), was the first great master of fantastic art, which could include such painters as Goya, Blake, Redon, and de Chirico, as well as the antirational Dadaists and Surrealists.

FAT-OVER-LEAN. The expression describes a basic principle for obtaining better permanence in paintings; namely, the overlying or upper layers of paint are to be increasingly more "fatty" and contain more oil than the layers they cover, or the "leaner" ones. This method assists in the adherence of the paint layers and insures that flexibility, expansion, and contraction will be on top of more rigid layers. This principle is especially important in mixed techniques.

FAUVISM (FOH-vizm). (Fr.) Refers to the group of French painters who, about 1905, rebelled against academic art and became known as "Les Fauves" (the wild beasts). At various times over a period of three years their work had a similarity, characterized by bright pure complementary colors. Somewhat emotional brushwork, deriving from van Gogh, was used in flattened space and simplified design. Matisse (1869–1954) is considered to be a leader in the group, which contained such painters as Derain (1880–1954), Vlaminck (1877–1958), Dufy (1878–1953), and Rouault (1871–1958).

FECIT (FAY-kit). (L.) A word placed after the signature of the artist on a painting, meaning literally, "he made it."

FEELING. Feeling is emotional responsiveness, as contrasted with the intellectual process of reason. In painting, feeling is an instinctive, emotional reaction to visual forms. The mind is constantly trying to organize the perceptions received through the sense organ, the eye; this activity, with feeling, is basic to the creation, experience, and appreciation of art. See also *Gesture.*

FIELD OF VISION. See *Linear Perspective.*

FIGURATIVE. Figurative painting is characterized by subject matter of recognizable figures, or objects. It also means representational, as opposed to abstract.

FIGURE-GROUND. The term refers to the complex relationship of "figure" (or the object) to "ground" (or the background). Usually, there exists a distinct sensation of

Ambiguity   Equilibrium (from Cézanne)

Two examples of the figure-ground relationship.

the figure being in front of the background; however, with abstract shapes, an ambiguity may occur in depth level when the background increases its importance and interest through conformation, color, etc., and assumes the position of the figure. The figure-ground relationship is of concern to the contemporary painter, even if his work is representational, as it involves an equilibrium between volume (figure) and space (ground), and their interaction with the two-dimensional picture plane. See also *Space.*

FIGURE PAINTING. See *Subject Matter.*

FILLER. See *Extender.*

FILM COLOR. See *Color.*

FILTERED LIGHT. See *Color.*

FIN DE SIÈCLE (fan duh see-EHK-lih). (Fr.) Literally, the end of the century. Used to describe the cultural atmosphere prevalent at the close of the 19th century, and suggesting considerable decadence and disenchantment.

FINISH. The degree of completeness of a painting as well as the final surface appearance.

FIXATIVE. (Also *fixatif*.) A clear liquid sprayed lightly onto charcoal, chalk, and pastel drawings to bind the granules onto the support and prevent them from powdering off. Fixatives are not used as heavily as varnishes, which form impervious films. Many different resins are used in fixatives: mastic, dammar, and shellac in rapidly evaporating solvents are common, as well as casein and the synthetic resins such as the acrylics.

FLAKE WHITE. A high-quality basic carbonate of lead. It is made by what is known as the old Dutch process, sometimes with modifications. In oil it forms a very tough and flexible film. It is opaque, covers and brushes out well, and is an excellent drier. Its disadvantages are: (1) It is cumulatively poisonous if taken into the system ("painter's colic"), but the danger is minimal if normal precautions are taken. (2) It will darken in the presence of sulphur fumes. This is a somewhat remote defect and not always irreparable. (3) It has a tendency to yellow, if kept in the dark for some time, but can be restored to its original brightness by returning to normal light. In spite of these defects, flake white is the preferred white in the oil medium, especially for grounds. In water techniques, it is unsatisfactory and should be replaced by zinc white or titanium white. Flake white is also known as lead white and Cremnitz white.

FLAKING. The separation of small pieces of brittle paint from the underlayers or from the ground of a painting.

FLAT. See *Mat, 1.*

FOCUS. The term from optics refers to the change and adjustment of the eye necessary for sharp and distinct vision. Even as the eye must change focus as the attention is drawn to objects differing in distance from the viewer, the painter can control that attention on the surface of his canvas by manipulation of edges, blurring them for an out-of-focus effect, etc.

FONTAINEBLEAU, SCHOOL OF. The influence of Italian Mannerist painting on French art was given considerable impetus by Francis I (1494–1547) who, besides inviting such painters as Leonardo and Cellini to France, installed several Italian artists at Fontainebleau, near Paris. A group of anonymous French painters, known as the School of Fontainebleau, was directly influenced by these painters.

FOREGROUND. The closest area of a scene. See also *Background*.

FORESHORTENING. The term describes the apparent contraction of an object as it changes from its most char-

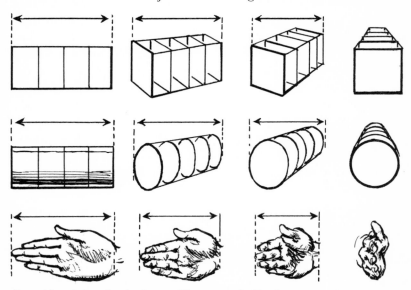

Example of foreshortening, with arrows indicating the two-dimensional contraction.

acteristic or extended projection to an oblique position in three-dimensional space. This modification is related to perspective and can also result in a three-dimensional diminution of size. The principle of overlapping is always present, and the two-dimensional contraction takes place on the picture plane. See also *Linear Perspective* and *Overlapping*.

FORGERY. A copy of a painting (or other work of art) that is made with the intent to deceive and therefore for a fraudulent purpose. See also *Copy*.

FORM. Basically, form is the configuration or structure either of an individual object or of an integrated group of parts—an arrangement. In either case, form is an organic unity involving the dominance of a thematic meaning. It is that quality which allows our apprehension of an object or structure, representational or abstract, usually existing three-dimensionally in space as a volume. See also *Volume*.

FORMAL. Of or pertaining to form. See *Form*.

FORMALDEHYDE. Used in painting as a preservative and hardening agent for glue. It is reduced to a 4 per cent water solution. *Formalin* is the name given to a 40 per cent solution of formaldehyde, which must be reduced with nine parts of distilled water to get the 4 per cent solution desired.

FORMALIN. See *Formaldehyde*.

FORMALISM. A term used to describe the strict following of rules or set ways or concepts of painting. The term implies an emphasis on form to the detriment of the content or meaning of a painting.

FORMAT. See *Picture Format*.

FOUND OBJECT (*Objet Trouvé*). A piece of junk, a

discarded object in which the artist feels there is aesthetic significance and which, therefore, he presents unaltered as a work of art. If the object is from man-made sources, it may be referred to as a "ready-made." Often several objects are put together and referred to as a "combine" or an *assemblage.*"

FRAME SIZES. Ready-made frames are supplied in standardized sizes. The size given is the inner rabbet or the size of the picture:

8" x 10"	16" x 20"	24" x 30"
11" x 14"	18" x 24"	24" x 36"
12" x 16"	20" x 24"	(Seldom larger)

FRENCH BLUE. Artificial ultramarine.

FRENCH CHALK. Usually talc. See *Talc.*

FRENCH ULTRAMARINE. Artificial ultramarine. See *Ultramarine.*

FRESCO. The term (from the Italian for "fresh") refers to mural painting and is of two types:

Buon fresco. True fresco painting. It is one of the more permanent forms of wall decoration. In brief, several primary coats of plaster are laid over the rough wall. Onto the last, the preliminary drawing is transferred from the cartoon. Then a final layer of plaster, called the *intonaco,* is applied area by area, day by day. On this, while still fresh and damp, the drawing is remade and the painting done. Such areas of plaster not painted, and on which a lime crust may have formed, are cut away at the end of each day. The painting is done with pigments ground in plain water, or sometimes lime water. Thus, as the water paint penetrates into the wet plaster, the color becomes an integral part of the plaster and of the wall.
Fresco secco. Painting on the dry lime-plastered wall

with a water medium of glue or casein. Sometimes the dry plaster is dampened with lime water before the paint is applied, but this is still considered *secco* as the plaster has dried and set.

FRESCO SECCO. See *Fresco*.

FRISKET PAPER. A fairly transparent paper prepared with an adhesive back. It is easily cut out as a stencil to be used with an air brush or spray gun.

FROTTAGE (fraw-TAHZH). (Fr.) See *Rubbing*.

FUGITIVE. A word used to describe impermanence in colors, namely, their tendency to fade.

FULLER'S EARTH. A form of silica or clay, fluffy and absorbent, known as diatomaceous earth. It is used as a filler in paints.

FUSION. See *Passage*.

FUTURISM. An Italian derivative of Cubism, manifesting a belief in the artistic superiority of industrialism and the machine. This dynamic and strident movement, with some Fascistic overtones, used techniques similar to those used in stroboscopic photography to get effects of speed and motion. Lasting from 1910 to 1914, the energetic development was quite removed from many of the qualities of its parent, Cubism.

G

GAGART. A term for Pop Art, coined by the critic Harold Rosenberg. An art gag. See also *Gimmick* and *Pop Art*.

GALLERY. A room or rooms where paintings are exhibited. The gallery of an art dealer is under his management and furnishes exhibition space for the artists he represents. Co-operative galleries are run by groups of artists, each artist sharing in expenses, exhibition responsibilities, etc. "Vanity" galleries are run as business enterprises in which the individual artist pays to exhibit. Institutional galleries are privately endowed or sometimes maintained at municipal expense; their purpose is always primarily exhibition rather than sales. See also *Dealer*.

GAMBOGE. A bright yellow color made from native gums. It is unreliable and impermanent, and has been replaced by cobalt yellow.

GARANCE. An older name for madder lake. See *Madder Lake*.

GEL. A jellylike form of a colloidal liquid. A mixture of linseed oil and mastic varnish, called *megilp,* is an example. The term is also used as a trade name on a "transparentizer" medium for oil color. See also *Megilp*.

GELATIN. See *Glue*.

GENIUS. A person of great originality and extraordinary ability, considered to be gifted by divine spark. In the case of the painter, there seems to be less emphasis on the purely intellectual capabilities and more on an unusual feeling for visual expression, with an individual point of view, and great vitality.

GENRE (ZHAH*n*-rih). (Fr.) Painting that uses everyday life as its subject matter, usually the life of the rustic. Genre painting differs therefore from the idealized grand style or the usual religious approach. The Flemish school is a good example.

GEOMETRIC. Pertaining to those mathematical and formal design elements derived from the lines, angles, planes,

83

and solids of the science of geometry. Opposed to biomorphic or free form.

GEOMETRIC ABSTRACTIONISM. An abstract or non-representational style of painting that uses geometric, rather than biomorphic, shapes. These shapes are two-dimensional and predominantly hard-edged. See also *Hard Edge.*

GESSO. Various mixtures of chalk, whiting, or slaked plaster of Paris, and sometimes a dry pigment such as zinc or titanium white. These are dissolved in a water binder of glue, casein, gelatin, or synthetic resin solution. Gesso is used as a painting ground or in a more pasty form for modeling, gilding, etc. See *Ground.*

GESTALT (geh-SHTAHLT). (Ger.) A school of psychology that holds among its ideas: (1) a part of a whole, through dynamic participation, alters its individuality in being that part; (2) all structural wholes have the attribute of self-fulfillment—in other words, it is not always necessary to supply all the parts to achieve the whole; and (3), any pattern of stimuli tends to be seen in the simplest possible way. The psychology is based on the theory that events or physical forms are not apprehended through the summation of separate parts, but through formed patterns made up of these elements; these patterns having more qualities than the sum of the qualities of the parts. The appearance of any of these parts of the pattern depends on its place and function in the pattern as a whole. Each pattern is called a *Gestalt* (pl. *Gestalten*).

GESTURE. The intangible line of life of an object, symbolic of the emotion it conveys. In a figure, it is more easily identified as a movement, or a state symbolic of an expression. In an object, the gesture is not what the object looks like, or what it is, but what its form is doing. This vitality or expression is felt by the sensitive artist in a sympathetic emotional reaction, or by the imaginative projection of himself into the form of the object by that process called *empathy.* Gesture also, of course, can be the action made to communicate meaning, as in the case of an actor's movement.

GILDING. The application of gold that has been rolled and beaten into extremely thin leaves. Gold leaf is fastened to the surfaces of panels by either a water glue (water gilding) or an oil adhesive (mordant gilding). In the traditional water-gilding process, the base is several coats of bole or clay (usually dull red), mixed with glue size. Upon this, when wetted, the gold leaf is carefully applied. The effect can be either matte or glossy (with burnishing), and the surface may be stamped to gain textural variety.

GILT. Gold leaf or paint. See *Gilding.*

GIMMICK. A term used to describe a trick of presentation, novel point of departure, or original and unusual graphic device. In traditional painting, an example would be the use of the reflected image in a mirror. In contemporary art, the gimmick is sometimes the only content, and often becomes an intramural joke or hoax with the intent of ridicule. See also *Pop Art.*

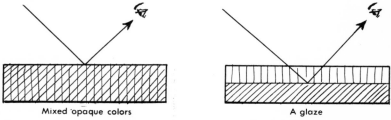

Mixed opaque colors   A glaze

Diagram showing the difference in optical effect.

GLAZE. A glaze is a mixture of medium with a transparent or semi-transparent color that is applied over a dried layer of another color. The resulting effect is optically

85

different from the simple mechanical mixture of the two colors. Glazing generally implies an ordered and carefully planned technique.

GLUE. Glues are used in painting mainly as binders in mediums or as a size in the preparation of a surface. Occasionally they are used as adhesives for collage, etc.

Casein. A glue, known from early times, made from skim milk. It is a tough binder in paints and grounds. Its films are fairly water resistant, but brittle, so it is not used on a flexible support.

Dextrin. This glue could be called a paste rather than a glue, and is made from wheat starch. It is used mainly as a binder in water colors.

Gelatin. A pure form of animal glue made from various animal tissues and refined under sanitary conditions. Its binding and adhesive qualities are not equal to those of high grade skin glue.

Skin glue (Hide glue). The best of this form of animal glue is rabbit skin, which is supplied either in sheets or granulated. The sheets are soaked in cold water, then dissolved by heating without boiling. In the ground form, soaking is not necessary.

Synthetic resins. The acrylics and vinyls are often useful in emulsions, as adhesives, and as binders in paints and in grounds.

GLYCERIN. The syrupy, oily liquid used to keep water-medium pigments moist.

GOLDEN MEAN. See *Golden Section*.

GOLDEN SECTION. Also called the *Golden Mean*. The division of a line into two parts in such a way that the smaller segment is in proportion to the larger, as the larger is to the whole. A rectangle based on this proportion (the Golden Mean rectangle) seems to be aesthetically

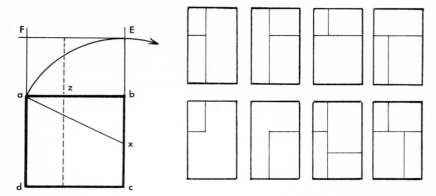

Variations on the Golden Mean rectangle.

satisfying. The proportion has been thought to have some mystical property, and an entire aesthetic system has been based upon it. To construct a Golden Mean rectangle, take original square abcd. Bisect bc at x. Next swing arc with x as a center and xa as a radius to cut the extension of cb at E. Then by parallels, complete Golden Mean rectangle FEcd. (In which, $Eb/bc = bc/Ec$; and if $cd = 1$, then $cE = 1.618$.) In addition, by making $bE = bz$, the rectangle can be divided proportionately.

GOLD LEAF. See *Gilding*.

GOTHIC PAINTING. Late Medieval painting of the mid-13th and 14th centuries in Italy was of two basic schools. The first was that of Sienese tradition, of which Duccio (c. 1255/60–1318/19) was a characteristic example. His work was definitely Byzantine in feeling, executed in tempera with considerable relationship to the miniatures. The other school was the Florentine, of which Giotto (c. 1266–1337) is characteristic. His frescoes depict figures, which, though set in shallow space, are strongly modeled in dark and light, giving them volume and weight. The

French Gothic, or so-called "international style" of
Gothic, was best exemplified by the work of the book
illustrators. Using techniques growing out of these miniatures, the brothers Van Eyck (Hubert, c. 1370–1426, and
Jan, c. 1390–1441), the founders of the Flemish school,
perfected the new technique of oil painting around the
beginning of the 15th century. Their work was characterized by brilliant color, spatial depth, detailed rendering
of form with the use of light, and concern for surfaces.
See also *Medieval Painting*.

GOUACHE. Essentially water-color paint with a gum
binder, gouache pigments have considerable additives of
whiting or precipitated chalk to give them body and make
them opaque. The paintings are often done on toned
supports of paper, panels, and cardboard.

GRADATIONS. The steps, stages, or gradients separated
by intervals and existing in reference to a scale either
between black and white or between a pure color hue
and a neutral gray of similar value. Gradations are obtained by additions of black, white, or both (neutral
grays), or by color mixtures with a complementary hue.

GRAFFITO. See *Sgraffito*.

GRAN-DISEGNO. (It.) The concept of great design or
of monumental drawing.

GREEK PAINTING. (Called *Hellenic* when referring to
the area of the Greek peninsula, the islands of the Aegean,
and the shores of Asia Minor.) Greek art went through
many phases: Proto-Geometric c. 1100–900 B.C.; Geometric
c. 900–700 B.C.; Oriental-influenced c. 700–600 B.C. (with
a new interest in representation); Archaic c. 600–500 B.C.
(with sculpture as the principal form of expression); Early
Classical or Transitional c. 480–450 B.C.; Classical or
Golden Age c. 450–300 B.C.; Hellenistic c. 300–100 B.C.;

and the period of transition from the Greek to the Roman, which began c. 100 B.C. The history of Greek painting is tied to the art of the potter. The decoration of pottery was done in one of three basic methods: in the first, the figures were in a dark glaze on a relatively light background (the reddish clay of the vase); the second method reversed this, with the light figures on a dark background; while, in the third, the figures were drawn in outline against a creamy-white background. By 480 B.C., from crude beginnings, the Greek artists had developed into sensitive draftsmen who studied natural forms, but did not copy them. There was no attempt to reproduce an illusion of Nature, but to capture its essentials and to express them in a noble, idealistic, and universal way. Actually, no Greek mural painting still exists, but there is literary evidence concerning names of artists and the descriptions and praise of their paintings. Surviving, of course, are the vase painting and some mosaic copies, as well as the later Roman (Pompeian) copies to show us what must have been Greek painting.

GREEN EARTH. A natural mineral gray-green color, of iron and manganese oxides. It is transparent and of little covering and tinting power, with a rather slow drying rate in oil. A permanent pigment, it is also called *terre verte,* and has been known since ancient times.

GRISAILLE (gree-SYE-yih). (Fr.) Basically the term means painting in grays. In easel painting, it is an underpainting that is subsequently covered with chromatic glazes. Also, in stained glass and in enamels, the details and shading were often obtained by painting in *grisaille.*

GROUND. The basic material spread over the painting support to give a uniform, receptive surface for the subsequent layers of paint. Before an oil or an oil-emulsion ground is applied, the canvas or panel support is protected

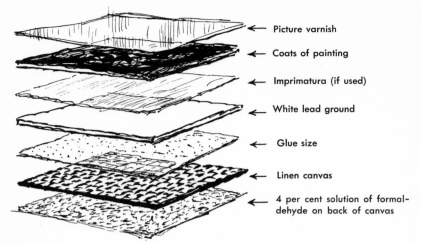

Picture varnish

Coats of painting

Imprimatura (if used)

White lead ground

Glue size

Linen canvas

4 per cent solution of formaldehyde on back of canvas

*Schematic drawing showing position of the ground
in the layers of an oil painting.*

from the action of the oil by one or two thin coats of glue
size. The ground can be only a single coat ("single-
primed") or a double coat ("double-primed"). The latter
is not necessarily to be preferred, as thinner grounds seem
subject to less cracking. In a ground of one coat, the texture of the canvas is more evident and gives a better
gripping surface for subsequent paint layers. Grounds are
usually white, giving an "inner light," or brilliance, to the
overlying paint films. (Those for gilding are colored,
generally a reddish hue.) Grounds may be of various types,
depending upon the technique to be used:

Emulsion ("half-oil" or "half-chalk") grounds. A mixture of gesso and oil, with the disadvantages of both.
Gesso grounds. Various mixtures of whiting, chalk, etc.,
with zinc or titanium white in an aqueous solution of glue.
Good for water-color techniques, tempera, and wax; for
oil, an isolating coat of glue or varnish is needed to render

90

them less absorbent. Gesso grounds are brittle and are only applied to rigid supports.

Oil grounds. White lead, thinned, with turpentine; a tough, flexible, elastic ground for oil techniques. Other pigments such as titanium or zinc may be whiter, but are not as durable.

Pre-mixed grounds. In dry form, with dry glue, whiting and zinc or titanium white to which water is added; or in liquid form, when the binder is casein or a synthetic resin such as acrylic.

The term ground also refers to the background in the figure-ground relationship. See *Figure-Ground*.

GROUND LINE. See *Linear Perspective*.

GROUND PLANE. See *Linear Perspective*.

GROUP EXHIBITION. See *Exhibition*.

GUÉRIDON (geh-ree-DOH*n*). (Fr.) A small round pedestal table sometimes used to support the objects in a still life, and also given as the title of the painting.

GUIGNET'S GREEN. See *Viridian*.

GUM. There are two principal gums: (1) Gum Arabic is a water soluble product of various trees. The best comes from Africa. It is used mainly as a binder in water color or gouache. (2) Gum Tragacanth, obtained from various shrubs, is used as a binder for pastels and chalk crayons.

GYPSUM. Native calcium sulphate. An inert white pigment, it is added as an adulterant to oil paint, and also used in grounds. When roasted, it becomes plaster of Paris, which, when slaked, is also used in grounds.

H

HALATION. The spreading quality of light that makes a light color area appear larger than a dark color area of the same size. See also *Diffusion.*

Example of apparent size difference due to halation.

HALF TINT. Same as a tint. See *Tint.*

HALF TONE. In the scale from white to black, any gradation of value that is in between—therefore, a gray. And, when used in referring to color, any gradation of value, hue, or intensity. See also *Tone.*

HANDLING. See *Brushwork* and *Paint Quality.*

HANSA YELLOW. The trade name for a synthetic lake, bright and of strong tinting strength. It is also combined with blues to make brilliant yellow greens. Recently developed (1934) from coal tar, this pigment seems to be quite permanent.

HARD EDGE. A term used to describe a style of abstract painting characterized by a precise, clean, geometrical division of planes and, often, by pure colors. In antithesis to the "lost-and-found" contours of the more painterly approach, the hard edge is in the tradition of *De Stijl,* and

92

its principles of abstract geometric design. See *Stijl, De* and *Lost-and-Found Contours.*

HARMONY. A factor in art meaning the integration of parts with each other and with their connected whole to form a unity, giving aesthetic pleasure. Although certain canons of proportion, rules of composition, etc., have been advanced, no formula can produce harmony. It has been said to lie somewhere between repetitive monotony and contrasting discord, and can be something as simple as the combination of similar, related units.

HARRISON RED. A brilliant red made from aniline dyestuff, having little or no lake base. Impermanent and generally unreliable.

HATCHING. A method of obtaining a tone by drawing a series of parallel lines; cross-hatching is shading with two sets of parallel lines, one set crossing the other.

Examples of hatching and crosshatching.

HELLENIC PAINTING. See *Greek Painting* and *Hellenistic Art*.

HELLENISTIC ART. The period of Greek Art during which the city states of Greece forfeited their supremacy to Alexandria, in Africa; to Antioch, in Syria; and to Pergamon, in Asia Minor. Athens fell in the 3rd century B.C., and during the Hellenistic period the Greek arts spread throughout the civilized world from Italy to India. This marked the emergence of Greco-Roman Art.

HEMP. A fiber used as a fabric for a painting support. See *Canvas*.

HERMETIC. Used in contemporary art criticism, the term denotes the cryptic self-contained reality of the artist's inner world; the word is associated with the magic of alchemy—the power of transforming, through psychic improvisation, the ordinary into the more precious.

HEROIC. In painting, the term is sometimes applied to figures that are considerably larger than life-size, and are thus of "heroic proportions."

HIDE GLUE. See *Glue*.

HIGH. A descriptive term used in the history of art to indicate the flowering of a period, or when its style is most characteristic. For example, one speaks of the Early Gothic period, the High Gothic period, and the Late Gothic period.

HIGHLIGHT. The area at the apex or crest of a form situated halfway between the light source and the viewer. The color of the form at this point will be its lightest and will approach its complementary color when it reflects a white light. A bright light source will produce highlights even on a very dark color, if the surface is shiny as metal

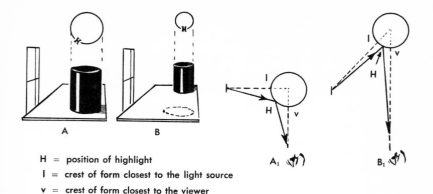

H = position of highlight
I = crest of form closest to the light source
v = crest of form closest to the viewer

An example of the change of position of a highlight.

or glass. Highlights are accentuated on moist surfaces, such as the eyeball, and reflect the color of the light source.

HOOKER'S GREEN. An older variety, sometimes called Prussian green, is made of a mixture of Prussian blue and gamboge, and is highly unreliable; however, the newer replacement made of phthalo blue and cobalt yellow or cadmium yellow is permanent.

HORIZON. See *Linear Perspective*.

HORS CONCOURS (ohr kohn-KOOR). (Fr.) The expression means "out of the competition." The *Concours* takes its name from the competitive student exhibition held at the end of a term at a 19th-century French art academy.

HUDSON RIVER SCHOOL. The name given to a small group of American Romantic landscape painters who, influenced by the consciousness of their native democracy and its wilderness, turned their attention to painting the Catskills, the Adirondacks, the White Mountains, etc. Several, such as Thomas Cole in 1825, painted in the vicinity of the Hudson, hence the "school's" name. Other painters were Doughty, Durand, and Kensett. Some were associated with the general movement but outgrew it, such as the panoramic painters, Bierstadt and Church, as well as the Barbizon-influenced, George Inness.

HUE. See *Color.*

HYDROSCOPICITY. The property of absorbing moisture from the air. Glue and gelatin are especially susceptible to this, and will expand as a result. To a certain extent, they can be hardened to reduce this effect by being sprayed with a tanning agent such as a 4 per cent solution of formaldehyde.

I

ICON. A painted image or representation, usually a portrait. In the Orthodox Eastern Church, it refers to that of Christ, the Virgin, or a saint, painted on a panel.

ICONOGRAPHY. The study of, and concern with, the subject matter depicted and its meaning in works of art, rather than with their form. The traditional manner of representing a subject, governed by more or less fixed rules and symbols, has unique meaning in each different field of study. One of these might be early Christian iconography, for example, or the iconography of Goya's portraits, etc.

IDEAL ART. See *Idealism.*

IDEALISM. (Also *Ideal Art.*) An approach to art in which the artist attempts to universalize and glorify his subject by conforming to an idea or a perfected ideal of it. Idealism is related to the Classical and appears in the conflict between Neo-Classicism and Realism in France in the 1850's.

IDIOM. Characteristic language. See *Visual Idiom.*

ILLUSION. Simply, the term *illusion* refers in painting to something that appears to be, yet in actuality is not. Thus, an optical illusion is a delusion.

ILLUSIONISM. The effort to reproduce the illusion of the real object. All techniques and means are used to delude the viewer into thinking that the visual is real. Sometimes referred to as *trompe-l'œil.*

ILLUSTRATION. Pictorial elucidation and informative description. Illustration tries to imitate and reproduce the visual anecdote; it is picture-making related to visual reality.

ILLUSTRATION BOARD. Made of drawing paper of various weights and finishes glued to a rigid carboard. The best quality is a heavy 100 per cent rag content paper on a superior backing board. The surfaces are usually of different textures: "Hot Pressed" (HP), which is very smooth; "Cold Pressed" (CP), which has some texture; and "Rough."

ILLUSTRATIVE. In the manner of an illustration.

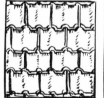

Examples of imbrication.

IMBRICATION. The decorative effect of the overlapping of edges, as those of tiles, shingles, or fish scales.

IMMEDIACY. A term used to describe the condition existing when the communication of the content and meaning of a painting are in no way hampered by the considerations of the methods of that communication.

IMPASTO. (Pl. *Impasti*) (It.) Paint applied in a heavy pastelike consistency, which leaves a raised textural surface and heavy marks of the brush or painting knife.

IMPRESSIONISM. Named in 1874, this was a movement in modern French painting deriving from Naturalism, and having as its aim the analysis and recording of the exact value and color of what the eye sees. Theoretically, the artist was to be impartially concerned with this rendering of the airy light playing over surfaces, without conceptual regard for the weights, tensions, and volumes of forms, or of their linear contour. Feeling and content were subordinated to the perceptual study of light, its vibration, refraction, and reflection, and its composition of pure hues; and of warm and cool colors. To paint only the visual experience was the aim, and not that which the mind knows. Detail was sacrificed to the allover impact, and a technique was developed of patches of pure color put down spontaneously (*alla prima*) while in the presence of the *motif* (usually the landscape) *en plein air*. By definition, this excludes the traditional prolonged study and compositional planning and development of the painting. The painters who were closest to the spirit of Impressionism were Monet (1840–1926), Pissarro (1830–1903), Renoir (1841–1919), and Sisley (1839–1899). Others, who were associated with and exhibited with the Impressionists at one time or another, include Manet, Degas, Cézanne, Seurat, Lautrec, Morisot, van Gogh, and Gauguin. When not used to refer specifically to the movement itself, Impressionism can be related to the work of artists of previous times such as Hals and Turner, as well as to more contemporary painters. See also *Neo-Impressionism* and *Post-Impressionism*.

IMPRIMATURA (im-pree-mah-TOO-rah). (It.) A thin glaze or veil of color brushed or rubbed over the white of a ground, relieving the eye of the bright monotony of the ground and unifying the subsequent painting. It may also be used at the same time to reduce, if necessary, the absorbency of the ground. An *imprimatura* is somewhat different from an underpainting, which is usually done more opaquely in the form of a composition and often in several colors.

IMPROVISATION. The process of creating extemporaneously and spontaneously, without plan, previous concept, or idea. Although present to a certain extent in all painting, improvisation has become, in some contemporary styles, the predominant method of working.

INDIA INK. A very permanent, waterproof, black ink made from lamp black.

INDIAN RED. Originally a native red iron oxide, it is now artificially produced. It is bluish-red and is grouped with the so-called "earth colors." Permanent.

INDIAN YELLOW. An obsolete lake color, it was originally made from the urine of East Indian cows. Being unreliable, it was replaced by coal-tar colors, which also were not satisfactory. Now, the best seemingly permanent color to replace it is Hansa yellow.

INDIGO. A deep blue, approaching blue violet. Originally, it was obtained from natural organic sources; now, from coal-tar derivatives. Both pigments are fugitive.

INNOVATORS AND DEVELOPERS. A combination of terms often used to describe the progression of various movements in painting as a result of the activity of two different types of individuals. First are the innovators, or the true creative geniuses, who change the direction of painting by producing an original style and introducing a completely new approach. Then there are the developers, who are under the influence of the innovators. Although without the originality of the innovators, the developers proceed to explore, elaborate, and solidify the innovators' contributions.

INPAINTING. In restoring, inpainting is the repainting, or the filling in, of areas of flaked-off paint and otherwise damaged paint layers. See also *Restoration*.

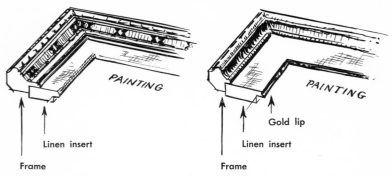

Frame   Linen insert   PAINTING

Frame   Linen insert   Gold lip   PAINTING

INSERT. An inner section set into a frame. Inserts are usually covered with natural linen, sometimes with a white or gold leaf lip.

IN SITU. (L.) The term describes something being in its natural or originally intended position or place.

INSPIRATION. A word usually avoided. It was associated with the Muse of the poet, implying an infusion of divine power that gave the painter his first creative impetus. A possible substitute is the less literary word, "motivation."

INTENSITY. See *Color*.

INTERIOR. See *Subject Matter*.

INTERNATIONAL STYLE. A term used specifically in architecture to describe the style developed in Europe in the decade of the 1920's, a style that spread throughout the world. The work of Gropius and Le Corbusier are examples. Also, a term loosely used in referring to any recognizable contemporary style of painting, which is indistinguishable throughout the art centers of the world.

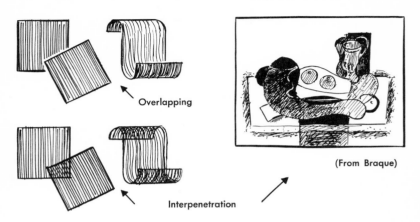

Overlapping

Interpenetration

(From Braque)

INTERPENETRATION. The term is applied to the mutually entering into each other of two colors, two planes, etc. Interpenetration may give an effect of transparency and produce an ambiguous depth relationship, which is in contrast to that obtained by overlapping. See also *Overlapping*.

INTERVAL. The space between periodic recurrences of

Example of interval producing movement. (FROM BRUEGHEL)

such elements as line, shape, or color. If the interval remains constant, rhythm is created; if it increases or decreases, progression and direction occur. Depth can be indicated by the combination of decreasing interval along with a decrease of size and intensity. In all cases, movement is present and tension is introduced.

INTIMISM. Scarcely a movement, it refers to the somewhat Impressionist painting of the "Intimists," such as Bonnard (1867–1947) and Vuillard (1868–1940). These artists were so labeled because their work was gentle, colorful, and reflected the quality of domestic life in interiors. See *Nabis, Les.*

INTONACO. A final layer of plaster in fresco painting. See *Fresco.*

INTUITIVE. Characterized by intuition, which is "the power of knowing, or the knowledge obtained without recourse to inference or reasoning; innate or instinctive knowledge" (Webster).

INVITATIONAL EXHIBITION. See *Exhibition.*

ISLAMIC PAINTING. See *Persian Painting.*

IVORY BLACK. An impure carbon black, originally made by charring ivory—now, animal bones. Permanent, but a very slow drier, and sometimes with a tendency to produce cracking when painted over. Cooler than lamp black, it is perhaps the black most commonly used.

J

JAPAN COLORS. An ambiguous term applied to various quick-drying, brilliant-hued paints. Some are enamels, drying with a high gloss, and made to be used on metal, etc.; some contain a resin varnish for sign writers, etc. None is included in the permanent palette.

JUGENDSTIL (YOO-gehn-shteel). (Ger.) In Germany, this was a movement associated with *Art Nouveau.* The name came from a magazine (*Jungend,* meaning "Youth"), first published in 1896 in Munich. See *Art Nouveau.*

JURIED EXHIBITION. See *Exhibition.*

JUTE. A fiber used as a fabric for a painting support. See *Canvas.*

JUXTAPOSITION. A placing, or being placed side by side.

K

KAOLIN. (Also called *China clay.*) A pure clay, native hydrated aluminum silicate, used as a filler or adulterant in paint, also as a base for lake colors.

KEY. A word often used to describe the relative overall lightness or darkness of a painting. A picture having much light and many bright colors is said to have been painted in a "high key." Inversely, with dark, deep colors, gloomy background, etc., the picture would be in a "low key." The color key is the basic color "note," as it is related to this overall tonality.

KEY, STRETCHER. Stretcher keys are small triangular wedges of wood that are slipped into the slots in the ends of the stretcher strips where they join at the corners. They can be driven into the slots to force the strips apart, tightening the canvas. See also *Stretcher.*

KINESTHETIC. The word used to describe the sense involved in the muscles, tendons, and joints, which is stimulated by bodily tensions, movements, etc. Concepts concerning form, weight, gravity, and movement in perceived objects, either real or painted, can be directly influenced by the kinesthetic or muscle sense.

KINETIC. Of, or pertaining to, motion or movement.

KITSCH (kitch). (Ger.) Worthless finery, or gaudy trash; the term is applied to the conscious appeal to bourgeois taste.

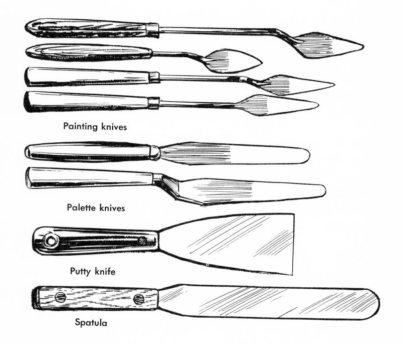

Painting knives

Palette knives

Putty knife

Spatula

KNIVES.

Painting knives. Thin, delicate, tempered steel blades of various shapes and sizes. The shafts can be long or short and the blades either straight or angularly offset.

104

Palette knives. Heavier, in varied shapes; used in manipulating colors on the palette, or for applying grounds to canvas, etc.

Putty knives. Used for scraping paint, plastering frames, etc.

Spatulas (or Paint knives). Large palette knives with straight blades used in mixing pigments.

L

LACQUER. Modern lacquers are made of cellulose materials and are tough and quick drying. They are used intensively for coating industrial products but seldom in permanent artistic painting.

LACUNAE. (pl.) (L.) A term used in restoring, referring to the areas of blank space in a painting due to flaked off or otherwise damaged paint. These areas are generally recessed and care must be taken in bringing the surface up to the level of the surrounding paint by regrounding and adding new paint layers.

LAKE. A pigment made by drying or staining an inert material called a base or a carrier, usually alumina hydrate. The older organic lakes were often extremely fugitive. The modern dyestuffs are coal-tar products, and a few of the pigments made from them are considered sufficiently reliable to be included on the permanent palette. See also *Pigments*.

LAMP BLACK. A pure carbon black made from the soot of burnt oils and fats. It is warmer than ivory black and is a slow drier.

LANDSCAPE. See *Subject Matter*.

LAPIS LAZULI. See *Ultramarine.*

LATEX. See *Synthetic Resin Paint.*

LAVENDER, OIL OF. Once used to disguise objectionable smells, and also as a drying retarder. See *Retarder.*

LAY FIGURE. A mechanically jointed figure; a life-size doll or manikin. It is used by the artist in place of a live model in studying the pose, costume, drapery, etc.

LAY-IN. The first allover covering of drawing, masses, and areas of color, sometimes as a mere *grisaille.* Usually loose and scrubbed on, but with a definite relationship to what the final finished work will be. Also sometimes called the *blocking-in.*

LEAD POISONING. See *Toxicity.*

LEAD WHITE. See *Flake White.*

LEAN. A term used to describe paint that is comparatively low in oil content. See also *Fat-Over-Lean.*

LEMON YELLOW. A misleading name applied to any number of pale cool yellows, some impermanent, some reliable.

LIFTING. The manipulation of pressing an absorbent sheet of paper (or cloth) onto a wet paint layer and then removing it, carrying off some of the paint and giving the surface a particular effect.

LIGHT. One of a number of forms of radiant energy that theoretically travel with wave motions. These waves vary in length, forming a continuous series known as the *electromagnetic spectrum,* and range from the short waves of radioactivity, the gamma rays, x-rays, and ultraviolet at one end, to the long infra-red, radar, television, and radio waves at the other. Roughly toward the center are the light waves, or those visible to the eye. All of the waves of this

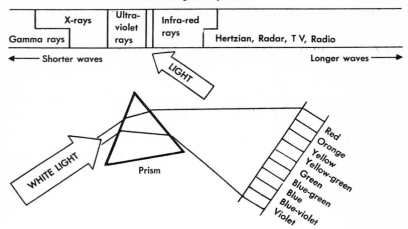

The Electromagnetic Spectrum

visible spectrum together form white light, which can be analyzed by refraction through a prism into its constituent radiations (the colors of the rainbow): violet, blue-violet, blue, blue-green, green, yellow-green, yellow, orange, and red; or a continuous color change between violet at the shorter end and red at the longer. See *Color.*

The term "light" can also refer to the comparative value of a color or a pigment, as in light, medium, or dark. See also *Light-Medium-Deep.*

LIGHT AND SHADOW.   See *Chiaroscuro.*

LIGHT-MEDIUM-DEEP.   Terms used with pigments to describe the range in the value scale and, sometimes, a change of hue. For instance, there is cadmium red light (which approaches a cadmium orange), then cadmium red medium (a mid-value), and then cadmium red deep (or dark, which approaches a cooler, bluer red as alizarin crimson).

LIGHT RED.   Originally a native red iron oxide; now, artificially produced. It is grouped with the so-called "earth colors" on the warmer end of the scale.

LIME (Calcium Oxide).   Used as a plaster and mortar in most of the early civilizations, except that of Egypt. The purer forms are used, when slaked, aged, and strengthened with sand and/or marble dust, as a mortar to plaster walls in fresco painting.

LIMNING.   A term used in association with the early American portrait painters, or limners; one way to describe any portrayal or delineation.

LINE.   Line is the course of the artist's point of attention as it moves through space, along intersections of planes,

Rigidly architectural

Scrubbed (stiff bristle brush)

Calligraphic (flexible pointed brush)

Manneristic (flat brush)

Examples of line.

108

across surfaces, and around the edges of shapes and contours of forms. The drawn line is a record of this movement and has such characteristics as direction, length, speed, degree of curvature, etc. It can be rigidly architectural; curving, as in natural forms; calligraphic; or manneristic. By manipulation, and with the use of various tools, line is used to express qualities of weight, density, and texture. It can convey the impression of fluidity, vitality, spontaneity, or hesitancy. Line records gesture. Often, lines of movement and the direction of tension and thrust may be only implied or suggested. Combined lines, such as cross-hatching, are used to create areas of tone. Line quality, per se, is the relating of such of these characteristics as are pertinent to what the artist wishes to express. See also *Linear*.

LINEAR. Pertaining to line. A linear style in painting is evidenced by the emphasis on the outline and contour of shapes and closed form, as distinguished from the painterly style, in which the emphasis is on the presentation of areas or patches of color and tone. See *Line* and *Painterly*.

LINEAR PERSPECTIVE. When the term "perspective" is used alone, it usually means linear perspective as distinguished from aerial perspective. Linear perspective is a geometric method of showing the appearance of three-dimensional volumes, objects, figures, as they exist on the flat two-dimensional surface of the picture plane or canvas. A simple form of perspective was first evident in the Roman paintings of Pompeii, about 80 A.D. It was not until the early 15th century that such men as the architects Alberti and Brunelleschi and, later, the painters Uccello and Piero della Francesca developed and formulated principles of perspective. Basically, linear perspective is concerned with the diminishing of size, the decrease of interval, and changes in direction, such as the convergence of parallel lines, all governed by geometrical principles. How rigidly the individual artist follows these principles is a matter of his aims, style, and personal wishes. There is, nevertheless, a commonly accepted descriptive nomenclature:

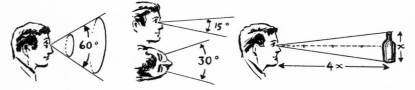

Diagram showing the cone of vision.

Cone of vision. (Also *cone of rays* or *field of vision.*) The spectator's range of view, in terms of angle. By moving the eyes, but not the head, we see approximately 60°. The fixed eye sees a field about 15° in height and, because of the two eyes, about 30° in width. We can see an object without moving the eyes and without distortion no closer than from a distance of about four times the object's height.

Eye level. The height of the viewer's eye, which always corresponds to the horizon.

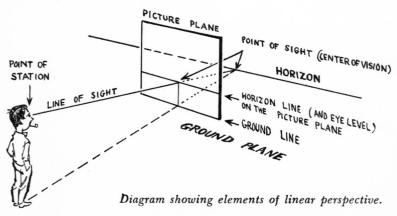

Diagram showing elements of linear perspective.

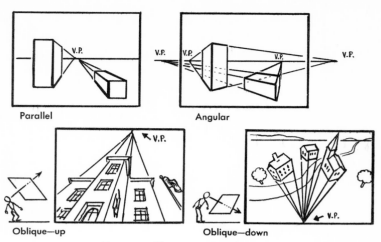

Types of linear perspective.

Ground line. (Also called *base line*.) A projected line on the picture plane where the ground plane intersects it.

Ground plane. The horizontal plane on which the viewer stands and which, theoretically, extends to the horizon.

Horizon. This is the line indicating, on the picture plane, the farthest extension of the ground plane. It is always at the height of the viewer's eye, or eye level.

Line of sight. (Also called *line of direction of sight*.) A line extending, perpendicular to the picture plane, between the viewer's eye and the point of sight.

Picture plane. The two-dimensional, flat surface of the canvas. Theoretically, this can be thought of as a transparent plane, upon which the various objects and forms in space are projected.

Point of sight. (Also called *center of vision*.) The viewer's eye position as projected on the line of sight "through" the picture plane onto the center of the horizon. This corresponds to the vanishing point in a parallel perspective plan.

Point of station. (Also called *eye position*.) The viewer's station point or eye in a fixed position at a certain distance from the picture plane.

Vanishing point. A point at which parallel lines, that are not also parallel to the picture plane, will meet if extended to infinity. For example, the extended lines formed by the parallel edges of a rectangular plane or volume placed on the ground plane will meet at a common vanishing point on the horizon.

There are three systems of linear perspective, depending upon the viewer's position and the basic number of vanishing points:

Parallel perspective. One center vanishing point corresponding generally to the point of sight, with frontal planes parallel to the picture plane. This is the simplest form of linear perspective, and the oldest.

Angular perspective. Objects are viewed on an angle with several vanishing points, but with all verticals remaining parallel with the sides of the picture plane. This is the system most commonly used.

Oblique perspective. This is a tipped picture plane, in which the line of sight no longer runs parallel with the ground plane. Horizontal lines may still vanish to points on the horizon, but the verticals will converge and vanish either up or down.

See also *Aerial Perspective.*

LINEN. Considered the best fabric for a painting support. See *Canvas.*

LINE OF SIGHT. See *Linear Perspective.*

LINE QUALITY. See *Line.*

LINSEED OIL. The usual drying oil employed as a binding medium in oil painting. It is made from the seed of the flax plant, which is processed in different ways to produce different qualities. The different forms are listed in general order of use:

112

Cold-pressed linseed oil. With no heating involved, linseed is crushed and the resultant oil is allowed to stand until the impurities settle out. It is then filtered. This is the preferred oil in which to grind colors.
Refined linseed oil. This is steam-pressed, refined, and bleached. It is more economical to produce than the cold-pressed oil and is the usual oil employed in color grinding.
Stand oil. Valuable in the painting medium, this oil is polymerized (having its molecular structure changed) by being heated without oxidization. It is heavier and dries more slowly than the other linseed oils, but forms the toughest flexible film, and yellows much less than other forms.
Sun-thickened oil. Thicker and a quicker dryer than the cold-pressed or refined oils, this oil has been partly oxidized, thickened, and bleached by exposure to the sun. It is of a honeylike consistency and is often used with turpentine in the final painting medium.
Raw linseed oil. Is heated before being pressed. The product is inferior and used only in cheap paints.
Boiled oil (blown oil). Linseed oil processed with heat and/or driers, and not suitable for artist's use.

LIQUITEX. See *Synthetic Resin Paint.*

LITERAL. (According to the "letter.") When used in relation to painting, the term indicates a matter-of-fact, rather unimaginative statement of actuality.

LITERARY. A term sometimes used in referring to anecdotal painting. See *Anecdotal Painting.*

LITHOPONE. Zinc sulphide and barium sulphate combined to make a somewhat unreliable white, used mainly in house paints. Also called *Orr's white.*

LIVERING. When an oil paint, on standing, turns into a rubbery, jellylike mass in the tube, it is said to "liver." This is most often due to inferior materials.

LOCAL COLOR. The term refers to the original and basic color, under white light, of an object. This is before it may be altered by the colors of a particular light source, reflected light, shadow, or atmospheric effects, etc.

LOFT. A loft is technically one of the upper floors of a warehouse or factory building. Usually large and well lighted, they are often used as studios by urban artists. See also *A.I.R.* and *Studio.*

LONG PAINT. Fluid paint, in which the brush strokes are smooth and flowing and the marks are self-leveling. Paint is changed to "long paint" from "short paint" by the addition of more medium.

LOOSE. The term is used to describe a painterly handling in drawing and painting. This involves broken patches of tone or color, lost-and-found contours, *sfumato,* and a free spontaneity in the strokes of the brush, etc. This is in contrast to the tight handling of a more linear hard-edge approach with careful delineation of shapes and forms.

LOST-AND-FOUND CONTOURS. A term referring to the painterly treatment of the contours of forms. These, in places, are softened and blended with (are "lost" in) the surrounding space, and also are sharpened in places (are "found") to give definition to the form. See also *Painterly.*

Tight linear outline   Loose, lost and found contour

LUCITE. See *Synthetic Resin Paint.*

LUMINIST. A term used to describe a painter who emphasizes light, using broken color in its full intensity with a minimum of shadow or darks. Especially applied to many of the Impressionists. See also *Impressionism.*

LUMINOUS. Brilliant, full of light. A painting can give this effect of light by both the predominance of colors in a high key and the use of the full range of intense spectrum color.

LYRICAL. (Also *Poetic.*) Terms borrowed from music and poetry, and used to describe painting in which the expression is basically emotional, imaginative, and extremely personal. In composition, another musical term is suggested—namely, rhythmical. The lyrical quality is basically a nondescriptive one.

M

MADDER LAKE. In many different shades under different names, the madders were lake colors made from the root of the madder plant. These pigments were highly fugitive and have been replaced by alizarin crimson.

MAGENTA. A fugitive lake pigment made from an aniline dyestuff. Also, the name given to a cool crimson or bluish-red color. This hue can be considered the primary red hue of the color wheel based on three primary paint hues.

MAGIC REALISM. A detailed super-photographic style of painting in which the artist attempts, through rendering objects carefully and in minute detail, to add an extra quality of emotional unrest and suspense, and to express elements associated with the supernatural.

MAGMA. A crude conglomeration of mineral and organic matter in a paste form. The word has been used in describing some contemporary painting.

MAGNA. See *Synthetic Resin Paint.*

Use of the mahlstick

MAHLSTICK. A wooden or aluminum stick about three or four feet long with a knob, once leather covered, on one end. It is held across the face of the painting as a rest to steady the hand for painting fine detail.

MALACHITE. An ancient color made from basic copper carbonate. It is a clear warm green, but not permanent.

MALERISCH (MAHL-er-ish). (Ger.) See *Painterly.*

MANDALA. A word from the Sanskrit used originally by Jung to describe the occurrence throughout all cultures of the circular composition with concentric elements. It has been applied to the rose windows of Gothic cathedrals, etc.

MANGANESE BLUE. The true pigment is made from manganese and barium. It is a brilliant, slightly greenish sky-blue similar to, but more transparent than, cerulean blue. It is a good drier and is permanent. Often, cheaper substitutes consisting of mixtures of French ultramarine or phthalo blue are mislabeled "manganese blue."

MANGANESE VIOLET. An artificially produced pigment made from manganese chloride and ammonium carbonate, it is a cool bluish-violet. A good drier and permanent in oil.

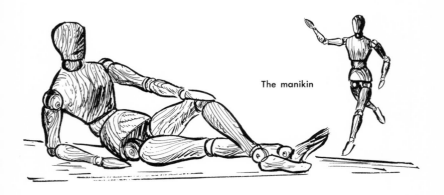

The manikin

MANIKIN. A mechanically jointed figure, generally smaller than life-size. Used by the artist in place of the life model to study the action of the figure, etc.

MANNERISM. (1) Overemphasis of a distinctive way of expression. Mannerism exists when the manner of expression dominates and tends to eclipse the feeling expressed; however, all personal mannerisms in the style of an artist need not necessarily be detrimental. (2) Mannerism is a term used in describing the period of Italian painting of the second half of the 16th century, when the rationality of the Renaissance was distorted and strained. It was not until the beginning of the Baroque period and a more vital return to Nature that, as a style, Mannerism waned.

117

MANQUÉ (mahn-KAY). (Fr.) Defective because of a missing ingredient. An *artiste manqué* is one who fails to achieve that which is expected of him.

MAQUETTE (mah-KET). (Fr.) A rough sketch or, more usually, a small model for sculpture. See also *Sketch*.

MARBLE WHITE. See *Whiting*.

MARINE. A picture having as its subject the sea or the edge of the sea. Also called a *seascape*.

MAROUFLAGE (mah-roo-FLAHZH). (Fr.) In mural painting, the method of cementing canvas to the wall, usually by means of white lead ground in oil.

MARS PIGMENTS. These are fairly new (19th century) artificially made equivalents of the burnt and raw native earth colors. They are made from pure red oxides, in certain cases with additives of manganese. They cover a color range from yellows more brilliant than the ochers, through intense orange and brownish reds, to the bluish reds as in Mars violet. There are Mars browns, as well as a Mars black. All are strong, intense, opaque colors, and absolutely permanent.

Mars black. Very useful, as it dries more quickly than ivory black or lamp black. It is a warm black.
Mars brown. Contains added manganese.
Mars red. Made in several different shades from red-orange to a bluish-red.
Mars violet. A strong but not brilliant violet.
Mars yellow. Iron hydroxide, similar to the yellow ochers but stronger and more brilliant.

MASKING TAPE. A gummed paper tape applied to the canvas as a mask or stencil in order to obtain clean sharp edges, as in an optical pattern effect. Cloth adhesive tape

118

of the type used in hospitals is also employed for the same purpose. A spray gun, paint roller, or the conventional brush may be used with the tape.

MASONITE. The name of the company that makes Presdwood. See *Panel.*

MASS. A simplified bulk or volume. Mass implies weight and attraction, or tension. See also *Volume.*

MASSICOT. An obsolete pigment made by heating and oxidizing white lead, turning it yellow.

MASTERPIECE. Originally the piece of work submitted by a medieval guild member to achieve the title of "master." It was the best that he could do and therefore his "masterpiece." Gradually, the word came to be used as any work worthy of a master. Now it has lost considerable explicitness, generally referring to a work universally regarded by authorities to be of highest quality.

MASTIC. See *Resin* and *Varnish.*

MAT. (1) Also spelled "matte," it refers to a finish or surface that is flat, lusterless, without shiny reflections—the opposite of glossy. (2) A mat is a frame for a drawing or painting cut from cardboard or matboard.

MATIÈRE (mah-tee-AIR). (Fr.) The material paint surface, with a variety of paint thicknesses, textures, and brush strokes. It can contribute greatly to the expressive quality of the painting. See *Paint Quality.*

MATTE. See *Mat.*

MAUVE. A violet lake pigment made from coal tar or aniline material. Very brilliant, but very fugitive.

MEDIEVAL PAINTING In Western Europe, it was restricted to painting in the service of the Church, taking the form of decoration of religious buildings and of the illumination of manuscripts. In the former, fresco and mosaic were developed with considerable decorative unity and respect for the two-dimensionality of the wall. Manuscript illustration was a combination of the classical ideal and a Byzantine decorative cohesiveness, plus a certain barbarous quality. Together with stained glass, it remained one of the most characteristically medieval of the arts, and continued to be most important until the emergence of easel painting in the 14th and 15th centuries. "Medieval" is a term that can cover both the Romanesque period and the Gothic period. The Romanesque qualities were conceptual, with considerable physical distortion and an aggressive spirit. The Gothic, or Late Medieval qualities, became more perceptual, more naturalistic, human, and milder. See also *Gothic Painting*.

MEDIUM. (1) The liquid binding material used by the painter on his palette in the process of painting. A pigment ground in linseed oil (oil paint) may demand as a medium a mixture of several ingredients: a form of linseed oil (i.e., stand oil or sun-thickened oil) with dammar varnish as a binder, and turpentine as a thinner. The word "medium" is sometimes used interchangeably with "vehicle." (2) Medium can also be used to mean the particular method or form of expression used by the artist, as painting, drawing, sculpture, etc. (3) In the graduation of color value, as in *light, medium,* and *deep,* "medium" refers to the middle values.

MEGILP. A buttery mixture of linseed oil and mastic varnish, once used as a medium in the early 19th century —with disastrous results.

MEMENTO MORI. A type of still life. See *Still Life.*

MERZ (mehrtz). (Ger.) The last syllable of the German

120

word for "commerce," which the artist Kurt Schwitters first used (by chance) to name his Dada collages in 1920.

METAPHOR. A form or shape denoting one kind of object or idea used to represent another, by way of suggesting some analogy or connection between them. Something that is used to explain another in a revitalized way and, in the process, obtains an additional meaning. Metaphors are continually used in painting to express complex feelings and abstract ideas.

METAPHYSICAL PAINTING. A type of painting with dreamlike overtones in what may at first seem to be a naive interpretation of life. Mystery, a melancholy isolation, and a foreboding sense of the unreal are present in changing perspectives, long illogical shadows, and strangely related objects. As a school, it was called *Pittura Metafisica* in Italy (1918–1921) where it was a reaction against Futurism. It is exemplified by the work of de Chirico.

METAPOLYMORPHIC PAINTING. A long name given to the type of contemporary Optical painting in which the picture changes as the viewer changes his position. This novel effect is obtained by various three-dimensional constructions on the painting's surface, such as a modified Venetian blind, an offset grill, etc.

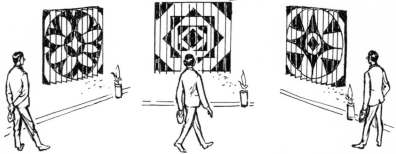

One form of metapolymorphic painting.

METHYL ALCOHOL. See *Alcohol.*

MÉTIER (meh-tee-AY). (Fr.) The artist's work or profession; that to which he is specially adapted.

METRIC MEASUREMENT. See *Centimeter.*

MIDDLE DISTANCE. The mid-area of a scene, which is between the foreground, the closest to the viewer, and the background or deep space. See also *Background.*

MILIEU (mee-LYIU). (Fr.) The environment; setting.

MINERAL SPIRITS. Products of petroleum sold under various names as "paint thinners." They are slightly cheaper than turpentine and, if desired, can replace it in all uses except in the dissolving of solid resins to make varnish and other products.

MINIATURE. Originally a small picture, illustrating a manuscript. The word has come to mean almost any very small painting, usually a portrait, thinly painted on an ivory support.

MINIMAL ART. The term used to describe a contemporary style of painting in which design, form, shape, and color are kept to a minimum. It consists mainly of simple geometrical shapes of closely related color shades of low intensity and contrast.

MINIUM. See *Red Lead.*

MINOAN PAINTING. That of the Aegean period, from c. 3000 B.C. to c. 1100 B.C. The primary examples of painting of the Minoan civilization are to be found in the frescoes from Knossos in Crete. Originally decorating the walls of the palaces, these frescoes depict athletic figures and animals, mainly bulls, with scenes of nature and aquatic life. The figures, with their pinched waists, large front-view eyes in pointed profile faces, have great vitality.

They are painted in bright reds, blues, yellows, and greens, with black, white, and gold.

MIXED TECHNIQUE. Refers to the combination of tempera (egg yolk and water) with oil (linseed or stand oil). There are several different methods of combining the two mediums: (1) the egg and oil can be mixed together forming an oilier emulsion and used directly, or (2) this same emulsion may be used to paint into a wet oil-medium color (wet-into-wet), or (3) the oil-medium color can be painted, usually as a glaze, over tempera that has dried as an underpaint. This last is probably the method least prone to problems arising from improper emulsification, etc. There are many variations possible in the formula for mixed techniques, such as using whole egg rather than yolk only, with additions of dammar varnish and/or Venice turpentine to the oil-medium. In all cases, the support for paintings in mixed techniques should be rigid, such as a sized gesso panel.

MODEL. (1) The person, male or female, who poses for the artist. (2) To achieve volume through the use of light and dark. See *Modeling*.

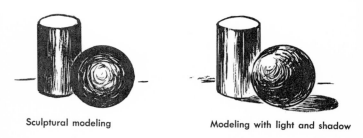

Sculptural modeling   Modeling with light and shadow

Two basic types of modeling.

MODELING. The use of light and dark and the gradations of half tones to give the appearance of three-dimensional volume and solidity. The two basic methods of modeling are by sculptural means or by means of chiaroscuro (light and shadow). In sculptural modeling, the lightest tone is on the crest of the form closest to the viewer. As the form turns and recedes, it darkens. Modeling with light and shadow, however, uses the characteristics of chiaroscuro, such as a definite light source, reflected light, and cast shadows. See *Chiaroscuro* and *Modulation*.

MODERN. Although the literal meaning of the word is "of the present or recent time, in contrast with an earlier period," it has become ambiguous in reference to painting. The term "modern painting" has been used to refer to contemporary painting or, as well, to painting since Masaccio (1401–1428); or, it may date from such diverse artists as Delacroix (1798–1863), Courbet (1819–1877), Cézanne (1839–1906), and Kandinsky (1866–1944).

MODERNISTIC. A bastard term used by the unaware in place of "modern." It might validly be used to refer, in a derogatory way, to the overdone and pointless geometric decoration of the 1920's.

MODULATION. A distinction is made between modulation and modeling. Modeling is the use of simple light and dark or shadow, and gradations of half tones, in order to give the appearance of three-dimensional volume and solidity. Modulation is more inclusive. While it also involves gradations of tone, it means the alteration in small gradations of the color hue and the color warmth and coolness in relation to an overall color key. As consideration is made of the whole picture, flat planes can also be modulated, and related as well to the modulations of the volumetric parts of the painting. Methods of color modulation are:

(1) Changes of the same color hue, adding its comple-

mentary hue for neutralizing and for the highlights (with white). In volumes, the more intense the color, the closer the form appears to be.

(2)   Changes in color temperature of the same color hue, "cooling" it as it recedes in space, "warming" the hue as it comes forward.

(3)   Use of different color hues, or broken color, to achieve depth.

(4)   In flat planes, modulations either of analogous color or complementary color.

(5)   Combinations of any of the above four methods.

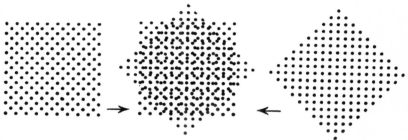

The formation of one type of moiré pattern.

MOIRÉ (mwah-RAY). (Fr.)   (1) In the graphic arts, the term means an undesirable pattern in process color half-tone prints caused by close to parallel angles on the screens comprising the print. Also, the pattern formed by the screen on a black and white halftone made from a previous halftone reproduction. (2) The term is also used to describe the pattern formed by combinations of allover screens, used for optical effects in Optical Art, etc.

MONASTRAL BLUE.   See *Phthalocyanine Blue.*

MONOCHROME.   A single color. A painting executed in monochrome would use only one basic hue, varied with black and white. See also *Grisaille.*

MONOTONE.   Of a single tone or value. Also used as an

inaccurate way of describing a painting done in one color, for which the correct term is a *monochrome*.

MONTAGE (mohn-TAHZH). (Fr.) A composite picture produced by combining several different pictures or details thereof. When photographs are used, the result is referred to as *photomontage*.

MONUMENTAL. In painting, a term that correctly can only be applied to pictures that are of the size, importance, and enduring qualities of a monument.

MOOD. The term, referring to a state of mind affected by an emotion, is often used in respect to the general pervading emotional atmosphere of a painting. The word *moody* implies a dark, rather depressing or melancholy quality. See also *Key*.

MORDANT. An oil adhesive used in a method of gilding. See *Gilding*.

MORTAR. A heavy cuplike vessel used with the pestle (a rounded stick) to grind paint and for general mixing purposes in the studio. Usually made of heavy glass or porcelain.

MOSAIC. A very old and durable form of wall and floor decoration, in which small cubes of colored stone, usually marble, glass, and tile (called *tesserae*) are set into the plaster or cement when it is wet. Modern mosaics are made with the same procedures that were used in the monumental mosaics of the Byzantine, Early Christian, and Renaissance periods. Also, oil painters may be said to use a "mosaic" of brush strokes.

MOTIF (moh-TEEF). (Fr.) The subject or subject matter and, therefore, the motive for a painting—its theme.

MOTION. Although the term is used interchangeably

126

with "movement," it could be restricted to describing the actual act of changing place or position, rather than the dynamic feeling of activity in a painting (which is called "movement"). See *Movement*.

MOTIVATION. See *Inspiration*.

MOVEMENT. In painting, visual movement is basically a matter of the changing position of the attention or focus of the eye. It can be controlled and directed by lines of direction, shapes, and tensions. Value and color relationships also influence movement. Obviously in a painting, change of position—motion—does not actually exist, but exists only in relation to the eye. It is through the progressive intervals of elapsed time as the eye moves through a composition that the dynamic feeling of movement is obtained. Movement is produced graphically in

Brushstrokes   Juxtaposition of volumes   Distortion   Phases of action

Growth pattern   Properties of matter   Gesture   Stroboscopic sequence

Examples of a similar visual movement produced in different ways.

127

many ways: in the brushstroke itself, as a record of the action of painting; in the tensions created by the juxtaposition of planes and volumes; in the tensions created within planes and volumes by distortions such as elongation, compression, twisting, etc.; in successive phases of action, either in the same object or figure, or in different ones; in associations with the growth patterns of living objects and the physical properties of matter. Gravity, weight, and position are all factors in movement. By empathy, the gesture of a form or what it is "doing" produces the feeling of movement through the kinesthetic sense. The viewer feels it in his joints and muscles. Besides the direction of movement, its rate or speed is also a consideration. This is based on the relationship of the ground or distance it has to travel. Although motion pictures may have influenced our way of seeing movement, the artistic means of producing movement in a painting are as they have always been. The representation of a running figure is more complex than the mere reproduction of a "frozen frame" of motion picture film. The stroboscopic sequence, the montage, and the simultaneity of multiple viewpoints have no artistic value in themselves but only in their use as expression. See also *Balance, Direction,* and *Tension.*

MOYEN ÂGE (moh-yeh-NAHZH). (Fr.) The Middle Ages.

MULLER. A lump of hard glass of three or four pounds having a slightly rounded bottom surface, and made to be grasped in the hand. The muller is employed with the glass slab in grinding paint in the studio.

MUMMY. An obsolete brown pigment made from ground-up Egyptian mummies. It contained, among other things, asphaltum and, despite its origin, was highly impermanent.

MUNSELL COLOR SYSTEM. See *Color Systems.*

MURAL PAINTING. Wall painting (or by extension, ceiling painting), either done directly on the wall or painted elsewhere and fastened in position. A painting can be called a mural, whether of fresco, tempera, oil, or mosaic, as long as it was made with the intention of permanently decorating the wall. The distinguishing quality of a mural depends upon this relationship of the painting to the architectural wall surface. See also *Fresco* and *Mosaic*.

MUTUAL SOLVENT. See *Solvent*.

N

N.A. These letters placed after a painter's name indicate he is a member of the National Academy of Design.

NABIS, Les (lay nah-BEE). (Fr.) The name taken by a small group of young painters in Paris in 1889. The group included Bonnard (1867–1947) and Vuillard (1868–1940) and had as one of its spokesmen Maurice Denis (1870–1943). They thought to spread a new gospel of painting influenced by the stylization, the flat areas, and decorative quality of Japanese prints. They were associated with the Symbolist writers, Mallarmé in particular, in insisting on the primacy of art over Nature. Paul Gauguin (1848–1903) and later Odilon Redon (1840–1916) were taken as their heroes before the group drifted apart in 1900. It was Denis who expressed their credo in his much-quoted definition published in his "Theories" in 1890: "It must be remembered that any painting—before being a battle steed, a nude woman, or some kind of anecdote—is essentially a flat surface covered with colors arranged in a certain order."

NAPLES YELLOW. A heavy, opaque, fast-drying yellow, made from lead antimoniate. Like the other popular lead color, flake white, it is poisonous; however, its qualities cannot be matched by cadmiums and ochers.

NATURALISM. Aspires to the representation of the "natural," without interpretation or change by the artist —actually, an impossibility. The term can be related to the photographic image; an accurate transcription of the particular, with exact measurement, profusion of detail, and rendition of form and surface.

NATURALISTIC. The term refers to naturalism. See *Naturalism*.

NATURE. "Nature is the system of all phenomena in space and time; the physical universe; an agent, force, or principle or set of such forces, or principles, viewed as creating, controlling, or guiding the universe" (Webster). "Nature is the existence of things in so far as it is determined by general laws" (Kant). More simply—for the painter, Nature is the living world around him, that world that he apprehends with his senses. The forces of Nature are translated by the artist into the laws of art.

NATURE MORTE (nah-tyoor-MOHRT). (Fr.) A still life. See *Still Life*.

NEGATIVE SHAPE. The term refers to an area of a painting that functions expressively only through its relationship to the dynamic (positive) areas or elements of

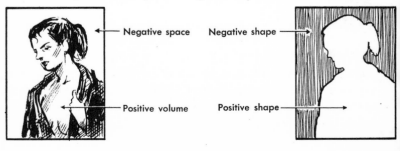

Negative space   Negative shape

Positive volume   Positive shape

the composition. A negative shape could be space considered two-dimensionally as, for example, the ground in a figure-ground relationship. See also *Figure-Ground* and *Space.*

NEGATIVE SPACE. A term used to emphasize the distinction between the physical emptiness of space and the mass of a "positive" volume. See also *Space* and *Volume.*

NEO– (Gr.) A combining word meaning new, or recent.

NEO-CLASSICISM. In the late 18th and early 19th centuries, there was a reaction by the energetic middle classes against the Rococo decorative style of the aristocracy. The excavations at Pompeii and Herculaneum and the publication and distribution of books and prints on the study of Roman art and history brought a revival of the Classical style. It was a severe, moralistic, and conscious imitation of the Roman antique. David (1748–1825) was one of the first and most creative of the Neo-Classic painters to use the Roman themes for the interpretation of current political attitudes. The success of the French Revolution in 1789 mixed patriotism with the official style of the Academy. David became court painter to Napoleon. Later, David's student, Ingres (1780–1867), became the outstanding example of the Neo-Classic school, with a tight, linear, intellectual style, coldly painted in spite of a sometimes lush subject matter. The Neo-Classic conservatism was opposed by the Romantic school, with Delacroix (1798–1863) as the major protagonist.

NEO-HUMANISM. See *Neo-Romanticism.*

NEO-IMPRESSIONISM. A more systematized development of Impressionism, founded by Seurat (1859–1891) in association with Signac (1863–1935) about 1885. Artists of the movement, following the physical laws of light and color, used a precise technique of painting with organized dots of pure related color. This was called *Divisionism* or *Pointillism,* and, with it, optical mixtures of more brilliant color were obtained. The Neo-Impressionists were also more concerned with the forms and structure of the painting than were the more spontaneous Impressionists.

NEO-PLASTICISM. An abstract movement founded in 1920 by the Dutch painter, Mondrian (1872–1944). Simple and geometric in style, it was applied to other forms of art besides painting, mainly through association with *De Stijl.*

NEO-ROMANTICISM. The name given to a rather sentimental type of painting of dreamlike nostalgic quality that appeared in the mid-1920's. The painters, also called the *Neo-Humanists,* included Tchelitchew, Bérard, and Berman.

NEUE SACHLICHKEIT (NOY-uh ZAHK-likh-kyte). (Ger.) New Objectivity. See *New Objectivism.*

NEUTRAL TONES. Tones without definite color hues, or with the hues subdued to the point that they register only as grays. See also *Color.*

NEW ENGLISH ART CLUB (N.E.A.C.). Founded in London in 1885, this group of progressive painters was against the conservativeness of the Royal Academy. They were influenced by Whistler (1834–1903) and by French painting, especially that of Degas (1834–1917), Manet (1832–1883), and later the Impressionists. Members associated with the group included Sargent, Sickert, and Steer. The organization grew fairly conventional; yet from it several other groups developed: the Camden Town Group, the London Group, and the Vorticists. In modified form, the New English Art Club still exists.

NEW OBJECTIVISM. (Ger., *Neue Sachlichkeit.*) A movement in German painting that originated in 1922–1923 as a reaction to French Post-Impressionism (as well as to German Expressionism) and resulted in a return to natural forms, realistically presented.

NEW REALISM. One way (European) of labeling Pop Art. See *Pop Art*.

NEW YORK SCHOOL. A group of painters generally associated with Abstract Expressionism or Action Painting who first made their appearance in New York's small co-operative galleries on East 10th Street in the late 1940's and early '50's. Although called a "school," their work is often quite individual and covers a wide range. See also *Abstract Expressionism*.

N.F.S. These letters following the listing of a painting's title in an exhibition catalogue mean "not for sale."

NIMBUS. The halo or disk of light behind the head of Christ, the Virgin, saints, etc.

NON-FIGURATIVE. See *Abstract*.

NON-OBJECTIVE. See *Abstract*.

NON-REPRESENTATIONAL. See *Abstract*.

NOODLE. To overwork by redefining, "correcting," and adding superfluous detail, losing in the process any expressive vitality. Also referred to as "tickling up."

NUANCE (noo-AH*n*S). (Fr.) A shade of difference; a subtle or delicate variation or gradation.

NUDE. See *Subject Matter*.

NYLON. Cloth made from nylon filaments has been used in very limited amounts for canvas. It is tough, but tends to stretch easily. As with fabrics made from the other synthetic fibers, it would seem to be most compatible with the synthetic resin paints.

O

OBJECTIVE. Pertaining to the emphasis on the external nature of the object observed. An objective viewpoint in painting is associated with the perceptual approach, as opposed to the subjective and conceptual. See *Perceptual Painting*.

OBJET TROUVÉ (ohb-ZHAY troo-VAY). (Fr.) A found object. See *Found Object*.

OBLIQUE PERSPECTIVE. See *Linear Perspective*.

OCHER. Any one of a number of native earth colors in a range of dull yellows, deriving their color from iron hydroxide. See *Earth Colors*.

OEUVRE (OO-vrih). (Fr.) Work; a painter's *œuvre* is the whole of his work.

OIL. As a term it refers to a painting whose colors were ground in oil and whose medium was oil. The oil is a vegetable oil—linseed. It is called a drying oil and belongs to a class of chemical compounds known as *esters*. See also *Linseed Oil*.

OIL INDEX. The term used by the authority Ralph Mayer for a rating of the relative volume of linseed oil absorbed by a pigment when ground to the consistency of average paste. This rating can be comparatively low, as in the case of flake white, or high, as in the case of viridian.

OIL-RESIN VARNISH. See *Varnish*.

OLEORESIN (or *balsam*). One of several different thick

134

resinous exudings of certain coniferous trees that are sometimes used in paint mediums and varnishes. The "oleo" part of the name refers to their quality of remaining in a soft semi-liquid state, until considerably thinned with turpentine and brushed to a thin film, or in mixtures in a medium. They produce paint strokes that are glossy and rich. They are:

Canada balsam. A domestic product from the balsam fir tree; often substituted for Venice turpentine.
Copaiba (or copaiva) balsam. A balsam from various South American trees. It may be used in restoration work, but never in painting mediums, as it is an extremely slow drier and is said to penetrate linseed oil films.
Strasbourg turpentine. A balsam from a Tyrolean fir tree, similar to Venice turpentine.
Venice turpentine. A balsam from the Austrian larch tree; has a long history of use as a glaze medium and in varnishes.

ONE-MAN EXHIBITION. See *Exhibition.*

OPAQUE. A term applied to paint with "body" that covers any underlying paint layer, rendering it invisible. However, all oil paints, with time, have a tendency to become more translucent (*pentimento*). Paint applied in an opaque manner, or in an *impasto,* has a different optical quality from that of transparent glazes. See also *Body Color* and *Glaze.*

OP ART. See *Optical Art.*

OPEN COMPOSITION. A composition that has the quality of the passing moment and the accidental arrangement, with a restlessness of free fluidity. The opposite of a closed composition. See *Closed Composition.*

OPEN EXHIBITION. See *Exhibition.*

OPEN FORM. A mass, loosely structured, into which

135

space may penetrate. Also descriptive of an open composition. See *Open Composition*.

OPENING. More exactly, the word refers to the pre-opening reception at an exhibition. Guests may be limited to invited friends, reviewers, and, in the case of group exhibitions, the participants. Refreshments are often served, sometimes lavishly. (Also called a *vernissage*.) See also *Vernissage*.

OPTICAL ART. The name given to a contemporary form of abstract geometric painting that uses a variety of visual phenomena and optical illusions. Important to optical painting are principles of simultaneous contrast, afterimage, intense complementaries, the interpenetration of shapes and volumes, color displacement, and the ambiguity of spatial relationships.

OPTICAL GRAY. See *Optical Mixture*.

OPTICAL MIXTURE. A method of color mixing used by the Impressionists and more systematically by the Neo-Impressionists. It involves placing small areas of different colors side by side, allowing them to be mixed by the eye as a mixture of light, rather than mixing the paint colors directly on the palette. Any mixture of color by glazing or scumbling or the use of broken color over an underpainting can be considered optical mixing. Optical grays can be complementary colors optically mixed side by side, or thin translucent scumbles.

ORNAMENT. Ornament may be considered any element in a painting that is an elaboration or enrichment, usually by regular repetition, of the textures, patterns, details, etc. What meaning ornament may have is limited to the meaning of that which it ornaments. In decorating any object, ornament may relate to the function of that object to such an extent that it can cease to be considered superficial. See also *Embellishment*.

ORPHIC CUBISM. (Also *Orphism.*) A further development on Cubism, mainly by Delaunay (1885–1941), in which the spectrum colors of Fauvism were used in large contrasting patches, while the forms were abstracted to a secondary role.

ORPHISM. See *Orphic Cubism.*

ORR'S WHITE. See *Lithopone.*

OSTWALD COLOR SYSTEM. See *Color Systems.*

OUTLINE. The bounding line of an area or two-dimensional shape. See also *Contour.*

OUTRÉ (oo-TRAY). (Fr.) Outlandish, extravagant, bizarre, or "far-out."

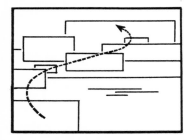 

Overlapping planes receding in depth. (FROM A.E. BARRON)

OVERLAPPING. The overlapping of objects, planes, or volumes used by a painter to achieve three-dimensional depth as well as to simplify grouping. In the use of abstract shapes, the effect of overlapping depends upon their outline, especially where they adjoin. Overlapping may be strong or weak. When it approaches the ambiguous, it may cease to exist, or it may become a form of interpenetration. See *Imbrication, Interpenetration,* and *Space.*

OVERPAINTING. Refers to any layers of paint placed over a dried underpaint. See *Fat-over-Lean, Pentimento,* and *Underpainting.*

137

OXGALL. Bitter bile from the ox, used for a wetting agent in water-medium pigments.

P

PAINE'S GRAY. Made only as a water color, it is usually a mixture of ivory black, a blue (ultramarine or phthalo), and a little ocher and white.

PAINT. Is the result of grinding dry color in a liquid vehicle or binder. It is mixed with medium and applied to a support of paper, canvas, or panel with brushes, knives, rags, etc.; this is done by varied manipulation to form opaque layers and transparent films that eventually dry, producing a painting.

PAINTER. In the field of easel painting, the painter is a creator. As opposed to the illustrator, he does not imitate reality, but through a pictorial act, translates it. His concern is primarily with creating an entity, not the picture of one. He tries to express his emotional reaction to life, not describe it. See also *Art, Artist,* and *Painting.*

PAINTERLY. (Ger., *Malerisch*—from Heinrich Wölfflin.) A term used to distinguish the style of painting that emphasizes the rendition of open form and surface by areas, or patches, of color and tone. There is a sensuous paint quality, in contrast to the linear style that emphasizes the more draftsmanlike approach of drawing, with line as contour. The painterly style is generally the more perceptual, more related to the visual experience than the formal conceptual style.

PAINTER'S COLIC. See *Toxicity.*

PAINTING. Painting is the creation of a possible work

of art by the application of paint to a two-dimensional support of paper, canvas, or panel. Primarily, painting is the expression, by use of visual principles and with visual elements, of the artist's intellectual and emotional reaction to life. It is one of the few remaining activities in which the individual, using a few simple materials, is given the opportunity to produce art; and this can be done, from conception to completion, without the dependence upon, or the interference of, any other person.

PAINTING KNIFE. See *Knives*.

PAINT QUALITY. A term that refers to the sensuous character of the paint application or handling. It includes: the brushwork, in all its variety of strokes; the differences in thickness of paint, heavy and opaque in the lights, thin and translucent in the darks; the use of glazes, scumbles, and broken color; the scraping, repainting, and lifting of the paint; the richness, oiliness of long paint contrasted with crisp, short paint; in sum, all the material results of the vital act of painting. Paint quality has aesthetic value when used as a means toward a more significant and profound expression and communication.

PAINT REMOVER. Any one of a number of volatile solvents either used alone in their liquid state or mixed with added wax or paraffin. (These materials hold the solvent in place and for a longer period of time.) In any case, paint removers should be used with care, and all traces of them removed or neutralized. See also *Solvent*.

PALE. A tint of a color that is of a lighter value than that termed "light." See also *Light-Medium-Deep*.

PALETTE. The term is used in two ways. First, it means the working surface upon which the painter lays out his colors (around the edge) and mixes them (in the center). This can be the traditional balanced wood palette held over the arm and grasped by a thumb hole at one side, or a table top of plate glass, heavy plastic, etc. Another use of the term is to describe the list of colors used by a particular painter.

Several types of palette cups and palettes.

PALETTE CUP. Palette cups are of different sizes and shapes (some made to avoid spilling). They are clipped to the palette edge to hold the medium, turpentine, etc.

PALETTE KNIFE. See *Knives.*

PANEL. A rigid painting support for easel painting, made of various materials such as:

Canvas board. Canvas glued over a rigid support, usually cardboard, is often referred to as a panel.

Cardboard. Unless it is of 100 per cent rag, cardboard usually deteriorates quickly. Academy board is a cardboard prepared with an oil ground in a textured finish in imitation of canvas weave.

Metal. Various kinds have been used, especially copper. Recently, textured and treated aluminum has been introduced.

Plywood. Layers of thin wood glued together with their grains crossed to reduce warping. Thin plywood fastened to a frame (as a door) has been used.

Presdwood. (Standard Masonite Presdwood; untempered.)

The trade name for a hard composition board used in construction and considered by many authorities to be the best of the rigid supports for painting. It is made of wood fibers with no added binder. It has a very small degree of expansion and contraction and needs reinforcement only in the larger sizes. This is done by gluing strips to the back, around the edges as a brace.

Wallboard. There are many types of cheaper wallboards, but most are unreliable.

Wood. The oldest and most popular support of any kind until well into the 17th century. Sizes varied from relatively small single pieces to larger dowelled and joined strips, which, unfortunately, often cracked. Wood is cellular, enabling it to absorb moisture and swell. Seasoning of the wood is therefore most important. Cradling and other reinforcing is often needed to prevent warping.

PANTOGRAPH. A mechanical instrument of jointed wood or metal arms used for enlarging or reducing drawings.

PAPER. Made of pressed interlaced fibers, paper is used as a support for water color and for drawings. The finest and most durable is made from 100 per cent linen rags. Other papers are made from 100 per cent cotton fibers, or of wood pulp. Surface textures vary from Hot-Pressed (Smooth), Cold-Pressed (Medium or Kid), and Rough. Weights are calculated by the ream (500 sheets of 22" x 30" size) and vary from thin (72 lb.) and fairly heavy (140 lb.), which have to be stretched, to very heavy (260 lb. to 400 lb.). Approximate sizes of water-color paper have been named as follows:

Medium	17½" x 22"	Elephant	23" x 28"
Royal	18 " x 24"	Double Elephant	26" x 40"
Imperial	22 " x 30"	Antiquarian	31" x 53"

The Imperial size is that most commonly available. Good

quality papers are watermarked; usually the preferred side carries the watermark so that it will be correctly read when the sheet is held to the light. Other types of papers used by the artist are: charcoal and pastel papers, available in colors; drawing papers in different weights and finishes; and assorted papers often in pads, such as bonds, tracing papers, and newsprint. Bond papers have the basic size of 17″ x 22″, with the letter size at 8½″ x 11″.

PAPIERS COLLÉS (pah-PYAY koh-LAY). (Fr.) Pasted papers. See *Collage.*

PARALLEL PERSPECTIVE. See *Linear Perspective.*

PAR EXCELLENCE (par ek-seh-LAHnS). (Fr.) Pre-eminently.

PARIS BLUE. See *Prussian Blue.*

PARIS GREEN. See *Emerald Green.*

PARIS, SCHOOL OF. The term has lost any specific reference to a single group of painters. The many interpretations now may refer to any international group after the Post-Impressionists that is, or was, centered around Paris and whose members are of the same generation. These contemporaries may include such painters as Picasso, Braque, Matisse, Bonnard, Miró, and Léger, or may be only the younger painters under their influences as Tal Coat, Pignon, Hartung, de Staël, Wols, Soulage, Mathieu, Riopelle, etc. Sometimes the School of Paris denotes those individual personalities such as Modigliani, Soutine, Pascin, Utrillo, and Valadon who did not particularly further the movements of their time. Still another interpretation of the term refers to a group of illuminators active in Paris in the late Middle Ages.

PARIS WHITE. The best grade of native calcium carbonate. See *Whiting.*

PASSAGE. The word is used generally to mean any particular area in a painting, but specifically an area where one form changes into another or into the background and merges without an outline. These passages are used to relate volumes or three-dimensional forms to the two-dimensional picture plane. Sometimes this blending is called *fusion*. See also *Lost-and-Found Contours*.

PASSÉ (pah-SAY). (Fr.)   Past, behind the times, outmoded.

PASTEBOARD.   Cardboard. See *Cardboard*.

PASTEL.   A method of painting with dry color pigment that has been molded with a glue binder into sticks or crayons called "pastels." The term is also sometimes used to describe the pale or lighter tints of any color as "pastel shades."

PASTE-UP.   A term taken from advertising art referring both to the process and to the product of pasting down ("up") various materials or elements to form a final composition. See *Collage*.

PASTICHE (pah-STEESH). (Fr.)   Extracts and details from a number of different originals put together in a single work. Also used as a term in forgery—a combination of elements copied from several different genuine works.

PASTICHEUR (pah-stee-SHIUR). (Fr.)   An artist who does not create originals but *pastiches*. See *Pastiche*.

PASTOSE. (It.).   See *Impasto*.

PATINA.   On aging, paintings acquire a patina or coating on their surface of yellowed, sometimes cracked varnish, which may also include dirt, fly specks, etc. There were periods when this "Old Master" look was highly valued, even though it might obscure the painting underneath.

PATRON. One who supports the painter by purchase of his work. Formerly, the Church and royalty were the artists' greatest patrons, commissioning many works. To-day, the individual private collector and the institution, often a commercial one, have taken over the role. The motivation for the purchase of works of art may be a desire for prestige or status, or they may be bought as an investment or because of true aesthetic appreciation.

PATTERN. The term is used in two ways: (1) to describe a designed arrangement or structure having an observable relationship of parts; (2) to describe a decorative, repeti-tive element existing as a textural area.

PEINTURE À L'ESSENCE (pa*n*-TYOOR ah leh-SAH*n*S). (Fr.) A technique of painting using oil color that has been drained of its excess oil by being placed on blotting paper, then diluted with a thinner, usually turpentine.

PEINTURE CLAIRE (pa*n*-TYOOR KLAIR). (Fr.) A name given originally to a method of painting used by Manet, and others, as follows: relatively flat unmodeled color in full illumination was put down in abrupt dra-matic contrast to the darks where the volumes turned. This was a simplification of the usual academic modeling of a full range of gradations of light to dark.

PENDANT. One of two pictures that exist as a pair. Also a drawing may match a painting and be spoken of as its pendant.

PENTIMENTO (pl. *Pentimenti*). (It.) A term used to describe a portion of a painting that has been painted over but subsequently begins to show through. This is due to the tendency for the linseed oil mixed paint on the covering layer gradually to lose its opacity.

PERCEPTION. The process of becoming acquainted

with, or the discernment of, something through the senses. A perception is a sensation; in painting, it is primarily visual.

PERCEPTUAL PAINTING. The emphasis in this approach in painting is on the images taken by the artist directly from Nature, rather than on any previous idea he may have of them in his mind. This implies an immediacy that is lacking in the purely conceptual approach.

PERMANENT PALETTE. A term referring to a list of pigments of proven longevity and resistance to change or disintegration under normal conditions of care. Although some of the following pigments (marked*) have properties that may disqualify them under unusual conditions, they are included because their attributes outweigh their drawbacks. A list for oil painting would include:

Blacks:	Mars, ivory, lamp.
Blues:	Ultramarine, cobalt, cerulean, phthalo, manganese.
Browns:	Raw umber, burnt umber, burnt sienna, Mars.
Greens:	Viridian, phthalo, chromium oxide (opaque).
Reds:	Cadmium, alizarin crimson,* Mars, Indian, light.
Violets:	Manganese, cobalt (phosphate), Mars.
Whites:	Flake,* zinc, titanium.
Yellows:	Cadmiums, Mars, ochers, raw sienna, Naples.*

PERSIAN PAINTING. The outstanding examples of Islamic painting are the book illustrations of Persia, the oldest of which date from the early 13th century. Few are religious; the subject matter is anecdotal: the legendary exploits, hunting scenes, etc., of heroes and kings. The style is two-dimensional, decorative, and rich in elegant and refined detail. In all forms of Islamic art, calligraphy is an important element.

PERSPECTIVE. Methods of representing the appearance

of three dimensions on a two-dimensional surface. See *Aerial Perspective* and *Linear Perspective.*

PESTLE. See *Mortar.*

PHOSPHENES. The luminous, moving, and abstract dots, lines, and shapes that the eye sees when the lids are closed and when pressure is put on the eyeball. These images have been used in the conception of painting somewhat similar to that of Optical art.

PHOTOGRAPHIC. Of or pertaining to the photograph. In painting, the term (generally depreciatory) means painting with the exactitude of photographic representation. The use of the term should in no way belittle the art of photography.

PHTHALO BLUE. See *Phthalocyanine Blue.*

PHTHALOCYANINE BLUE (Phthalo Blue). Also called *Thalo blue* and *Monastral blue* and by several other proprietary names. It is a very powerful, transparent, greenish-blue, somewhat similar in hue to Prussian blue, which it can replace. Developed as recently as 1935, from organic dyestuffs, it is one of the very few synthetic lake pigments that seem to be permanent.

PHTHALOCYANINE GREEN. A variety of phthalocyanine blue, approaching viridian in hue.

PICTORIAL. Of or pertaining to a picture or painting. Implies a recognizable depiction.

PICTURE. The visual representation—a term generally used interchangeably with "painting."

PICTURE BOX. A term used to describe the illusional or pictorial three-dimensional enclosed space of the picture, its front plane being the picture plane. The picture

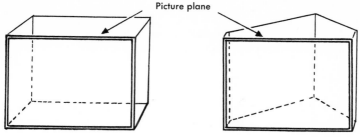

Picture plane

Two examples of the picture box.

box may be in the form of a cube, parallel to the picture surface or on an angle. A relationship of the enclosed pictorial space to the picture plane can create a controlled picture box of even deep space.

PICTURE FORMAT. The shape or proportions of the picture, be it square, rectangular, oval, etc.

PICTURE PLANE. The two-dimensional or flat surface of the canvas. Painting starting with Cézanne concerns itself with relating the illusional three-dimensionality of the picture space to the picture plane. See also *Linear Perspective.*

PICTURESQUE. The term has been used with a certain derogatory implication to mean simple tattered charm. Broken lines and tones, dim and shifting light, restless forms and masses, all assist in producing the picturesque effect when presented for their own sake. The picturesque has been characterized by the art historian Heinrich Wölfflin, who points out that, in addition to the particular effect arising from the complexities (picturesqueness) of certain forms, "over the solid, static body of things there will always play the stimulus of [an all-pervading] movement which does not reside in the object, and that also means that the whole only exists as a *picture* for the eye. . . ." He continues by contrasting the picturesque with "real painterly content." See also *Painterly.*

PICTURE VARNISH. See *Varnish.*

PIETÀ (pee-ay-TAH). (It.) Meaning pity or compassion, the term refers to the representation of the Virgin Mary mourning over the body of the dead Christ held in her lap.

PIGMENTS. Although the word is used interchangeably with *color* and *paint, pigment,* more properly, is the dry color in a granular state that is mixed, usually ground, with a liquid binding agent (called the *vehicle*) to form paint. This enables it, either alone or combined with other paint, to be applied to a support in a range of manipulations, from thin wash to heavy *impasto.* Pigments are of different types and are obtained from different sources. They are listed below in order of their general permanency:

Natural mineral pigments. The "earth colors" known since prehistoric times. They are mostly iron oxides, and tend toward browns and dull oranges, and when roasted or burnt become deeper and warmer colors.
Man-made mineral pigments. Made in color factories from various minerals and metals by chemical processes.
Natural organic pigments. Come from animal or plant life and are not permanent.
Artificial organic pigments. Man-made pigments, mostly from carbon compounds.
Dyes. Stains. Unlike true pigments, which retain their bulk and remain suspended in the vehicle, a dye dissolves completely. Some dyes are organic, some man-made from coal-tar derivatives. Dyes often have the objectionable ability to "bleed" (to penetrate and stain an overlaying or adjoining layer of paint).
Lakes. Inert materials called *bases* that have been dyed or stained to form a pigment.

PINXIT (or *Pinx*). (L.) A word placed after the signature of the artist on a painting, meaning literally, "he painted it."

PITTURA METAFISICA. (It.) See *Metaphysical Painting*.

PLANE. A flat surface having in itself only two dimensions, yet which may exist in three-dimensional space. Planes are diagrammatically rectangular, but actually can be of any shape. Joined together, they form volumes. A cube, for example, would be enclosed by three visible planes or six actual planes. A sphere is enclosed by an infinite number of planes. See *Shape, Space,* and *Volume.*

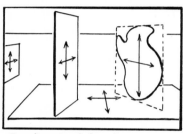

Two-dimensional planes in three-dimensional space

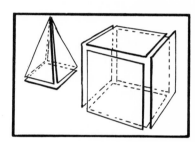

Planes forming volumes

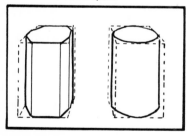

Formation of a cylinder

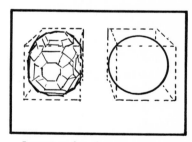

Formation of a sphere

PLASTER. See *Lime* and *Gypsum.*

PLASTER CAST. One of a number of reproductions in plaster of antique examples of sculpture. These are used in the study of drawing, formerly much more extensively than now. Usually reduced in size, they include such pieces as the Venus de Milo, the Winged Victory, and the Apollo Belvedere. Other plaster casts are anatomical figures and horses, and details of the human figure, such as the foot or hand, or the eye, ear, nose, or lips.

PLASTER OF PARIS. See *Gypsum*.

PLASTIC. A term used in referring to the elements and the means used by the painter in achieving a pictorial organization of expressive value. These are the planes, the volumes, the tensions, the weights, etc., as opposed to the literary elements, the anecdotal, and the psychological factors, etc. The term is also used in referring to synthetic resin paint. See also *Synthetic Resin Paint*.

PLASTIC ARTS. A term used to differentiate the arts using physical materials, and primarily involved with vision and space, such as painting, sculpture, and architecture, from the performing arts of music, opera, theater, and the dance, as well as those of literature. The Plastic Arts are also referred to as the Space Arts, or the Visual Arts.

PLASTICITY. A term more properly applied to modeling, but used in painting to describe the quality of apparent three-dimensionality.

PLASTICIZER. A material added to paints, varnishes, etc., to impart flexibility and better brushing-out qualities.

PLASTIC PAINT. A name used for synthetic resin paint. See *Synthetic Resin Paint*.

PLEIN AIR. See *En Plein Air*.

PLEXIGLASS. A form of acrylic resin. See *Resin* and *Varnish*.

POCHADE (poh-SHAHD). (Fr.) A small rough sketch, usually in oils, done from the *motif*; to be used later in the studio in painting a larger more developed version.

POETIC. See *Lyrical*.

POINTILLISM. See *Neo-Impressionism.*

POINT OF SIGHT. See *Linear Perspective.*

POINT OF STATION. See *Linear Perspective.*

POLYMER. A chemical compound made up of the same atoms as another compound, but of different molecular structure with larger molecules. Polymers have higher molecular weight and different physical properties. They are used in the synthetic resin paints and varnishes.

POLYPTYCH (poh-LIP-tik). (Gr.) A painting in more than one part or section. See *Triptych.*

POLYVINYL ACETATE. See *Resin* and *Varnish.*

POP ART. (Known in Europe as *New Realism.*) The name given a faddish antitraditional, antiaesthetic glorification of mass culture that blossomed in the early 1960's. As in Dada, effort is made to startle or surprise and to extract significance from the banal, man-made objects and trivia of everyday life. Appreciation for any aesthetic quality in Pop Art's products by its patrons is minor compared to the psychological security they achieve by identifying with the group that is currently popular. As an "art" movement, Pop Art has been commercially promoted and merchandized but, paradoxically, it may show the pretense in much of the advertising in mass media.

POPPYSEED OIL. A drying oil used as a binding medium in oil painting, it is pressed from the seeds of the plant. It is sometimes used in the grinding of white pigments as it has a tendency to yellow less than linseed oil. It dries very slowly with a film not quite as tough as that formed by linseed oil.

P.O.R. These letters following the listing of a painting's title in an exhibition catalogue mean "price on request."

PORTRAIT. See *Subject Matter.*

POSE. To pose the model is to place him or her in a certain attitude or posture. As a word of command, "Pose, please," commences the pose—"Rest," terminates it.

POSITIVE SPACE. See *Space.*

POSITIVE VOLUME. A term used to emphasize the distinction between the mass of a volume and the physical emptiness of "negative" space. See also *Space* and *Volume.*

POST– (L.) A prefix meaning "subsequent to," or "after."

POST-IMPRESSIONISM. Developing in the 1880's as a reaction to Impressionism, this rather loosely connected movement has been divided into two branches. As the individual Impressionist artists developed, some, represented by van Gogh (1853–1890) and Gauguin (1848–1903), stressed the emotional or expressionistic aspect of painting. Others, represented by Cézanne (1839–1906) and the Neo-Impressionist Seurat (1859–1891), emphasized a return to formal structure. From these two branches evolved Expressionism, on the one hand, and Cubism, on the other. See also *Cubism* and *Expressionism.*

POUNCE. In fresco painting, pouncing is one method used to transfer the drawing from the cartoon on detail-paper onto the wall. The lines of the drawing having been perforated with a perforating wheel, the drawing is placed in position on the wall, and dry color chalk, or charcoal in a small muslin bag, is pounced through the perforations, marking the wall.

POWDERING. A condition that occurs when an oil paint film is overly thinned, loses its adhesive power, and crumbles away. This may also occur when a highly absorbent ground draws off the binder, or when old paint that has lost its adhesive quality is used.

PREHISTORIC PAINTING. The earliest known paintings were done sometime between 14,000 and 28,000 years ago by Cro-Magnon man. Inspired probably by a primitive religion or hunting magic, these paintings are to be found in the caves of southern France and in Spain. They are depictions of bison, antelopes, deer, cattle, horses, bears, rhinoceros, and, rarely and more crudely, men. The early paintings were outline drawings done with charcoal and colored chalks. Sometimes the color was blown on (aerograph) through a hollow tube made of reed or bone. Later, the painter developed engraving and scraping tools and, rendering his animals more and more lifelike, used primitive brushes possibly made of split reeds, feathers, or even animal hair. The pigments were obtained from earth color: reds and yellows from iron oxides, greens from manganese oxide, while the blacks were carbon from soot and charred bone. These colors were probably ground on stone with oily animal fat. In all cases, the forms are isolated units and there appears to have been no effort to relate the animals one to another and no attempt at any form of composition. Other examples of prehistoric painting are to be found in the beginnings of other cultures, notably the Egyptian. See *Egyptian Painting.*

PRE-RAPHAELITE. The term refers to a movement in English art stemming from the Pre-Raphaelite Brotherhood (P.R.B.), founded in 1848 by Holman Hunt, John E. Millais, and Dante Gabriel Rossetti. The name was derived from the emulation of the Italian pre-Raphael painters such as Botticelli and Gozzoli. The paintings of the English group were literary, romantic, and sentimental.

PRESDWOOD. The trade name of a wallboard used as a rigid support in painting. See *Panel.*

PRIMARY COLOR. See *Color* and *Color Wheel.*

153

PRIMING. The preliminary coats of material spread over a support to prepare it for painting. These usually consist of a white ground over a coat of glue size. See *Ground.*

PRIMITIVE ART. That produced by tribal peoples who are without written language and whose culture is on a level with that of Neolithic man. There have been productive periods in Africa, North America, and Oceania, all before contact with Europeans. Examples of two-dimensional painting, per se, rarely exist, however, as most of the art is in the form of sculpture, pottery, weaving, and body ornament.

PRIMITIVISM. The self-conscious turning back for inspiration, by the contemporary artist, to the archaic forms of savage peoples. Although this does not necessarily imply crudeness in execution, it does indicate a directness, a spontaneity, and a nonintellectual intuitiveness. These qualities, with a strong mysticism, are usually found in the art of all primitive cultures. The difficulty lies in the necessity for the contemporary artist to imitate consciously, which leads to superficiality. The word *primitive* has been applied to schools of painting such as the Italian and Flemish before the Renaissance and is thus a comparative term. The naive art of children, as well as the quaint work of technically incompetent amateurs, has been described as primitive. All of the above examples are not to be confused with true Primitive Art, or the art of the savage. See *Primitive Art.*

PRISMATIC COLOR. See *Color.*

PRIX DE ROME (pree duh ROHM). (Fr.) The Rome Prize, an annual competitive fellowship for residence and study in Rome awarded by the American Academy in Rome. The term *Prix de Rome* is taken from the French equivalent awarded by the École des Beaux-Arts in Paris, for a year's study in Rome at the French Academy.

PROFIL PERDU (pro-FEEL pair-DIU). (Fr.) An aspect of the head in which the profile is lost because the head is turned away. The term is also applied to objects in similar circumstances.

PROJECTOR. One of several different types of mechanical devices used by some contemporary painters to throw an image onto the canvas where it can be traced. Opaque projectors can be used to transfer and enlarge sketches, drawings, etc. Also occasionally used are the transparency projectors for slides. See also *Camera Obscura*.

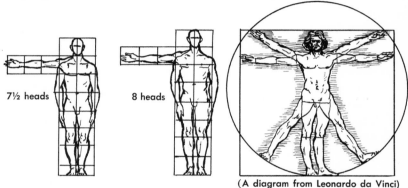

7½ heads   8 heads   **(A diagram from Leonardo da Vinci)**

Human proportions.

PROPORTION. One of the interrelating principles of design. Proportion is a comparison or relationship. It may be influenced by norms or averages, which arise from the ideals of different styles and periods in art. In the relationships between dimensions, sizes, amounts, intensities, etc., proportion is manipulated to achieve special goals. It is doubtful whether rigid absolutes govern these relationships; they become "correct" as they achieve the effects desired. However, the so-called Golden Section, a proportion of measurement, would seem to indicate some universal criterion. To the painter, proportion is a primary consideration most apparent in its application to the human figure. See also *Golden Section*.

PROVENANCE. A history or pedigree of a painting; the establishment of the identity of successive owners since its execution. Also included would be all published documents, catalogues, and journals that contain references to the painting, along with reproductions, exhibitions, and sales records, as well as correspondence, especially of the artist, in which mention of it may be made.

PROVOCATIVE. A term often used in art criticism. The word means the ability to provoke, stimulate, or incite. When used alone, it is ambiguous as there is no indication of what emotion is brought forth, even though in some cases annoyance or vexation may be correctly implied.

PRUSSIAN BLUE. Artificially produced from a complex iron compound, it has many other names, such as Antwerp blue, Berlin blue, Paris blue, and Chinese blue. It is a strong, transparent greenish-blue and in concentrated form is often recognizable by its metallic sheen. Considered to be only semi-permanent, it is often replaced by phthalo blue, which it resembles in hue.

PRUSSIAN BROWN. Originally made by heating Prussian blue, now the term refers to raw Indian red (iron oxide).

PRUSSIAN GREEN. See *Hooker's Green.*

PSYCHEDELIC ART. A projected melange of painting, photography, animation, electronics, and interior decoration aimed at producing in the "viewer" the hallucinatory effects and so-called mind-expanding perceptions that LSD, and other psychedelic drugs, create. Such actual painting that is used is often biomorphic or geometric.

PURE GUM TURPENTINE. See *Turpentine.*

PURISM. The name given to a movement derving from Cubism and founded in 1916 by Ozenfant (1886–1966)

156

and Le Corbusier (1887–1965). It emphasized precision, clarity, and the impersonal technological influences of modern life.

PURPLE. A color hue similar to violet, but usually considered to be closer to red than to blue; therefore a slightly reddish-violet. Purple does not occur on the visible spectrum, but in the color wheel it is placed between violet and red.

PUSH AND PULL. A term originated by the painter Hans Hofmann to explain the simultaneous interoperation of two-dimensional flatness and the effect of three-dimensional depth. This relationship is not used to create an illusion of natural space, but to create a tension that in turn produces an active plastic depth.

PUTTO (pl. *Putti*). (It.) Meaning "small boy," the word applies to the cherubs that appear in Italian Renaissance painting.

P.V.A. Abbreviation for polyvinyl acetate. See *Resin* and *Varnish*.

Q

QUATTROCENTO (kwa-troh-CHEN-toh). (It.) The 1400's, or the 15th century.

R

R.A. These letters, placed after a painter's name, indicate that he is a member of the Royal Academy of Arts in London.

RABBIT-SKIN GLUE. See *Glue.*

RAISON D'ÊTRE (ray-zohn DEH-trih). (Fr.) The reason for a thing's existence; its justification for being.

RAISONNÉ (ray-zohn-NAY). (Fr.) The word is often used with "catalogue" as in the *catalogue raisonné* of an artist's work. This means a catalogue systematically arranged.

RAW COLOR. A relative term used to describe strident or inharmonious color. (The adjective "raw" used with a specific color such as sienna, for instance, refers to the unburnt shade.)

RAW SIENNA. A natural earth color, it is a deeper yellow ocher. It is permanent and has been known from ancient times.

RAW UMBER. A natural earth color, it is a gray-greenish brown. It is permanent and has been known from ancient times.

READY-MADE. See *Found Object.*

REALISM. Following the conflict between Neo-Classicists and Romantics, the Realists (who included writers as well) rejected both movements and concerned themselves with the "real" life of their time. The effort was made to depict the real or the actual as it exists and is apprehended by the senses. Realism differs from Naturalism in the stressing of the convincing universal, without minute detail, rather than the particular as the basis of reality. Courbet (1819–1877) with "Le Réalisme" in 1855 avoided the picturesque, the poetic, and the sentimental and attempted to state, with detachment, that which he saw. Daumier (1808–1879) was a realist in this tradition, but of considerably greater power. Realism is not to be confused with Naturalism. See *Naturalism.*

REALISTIC. A term often used in place of "figurative" or "representational."

REALITY. In philosophy, the term refers to the state of being real or to that which has objective existence as opposed to an idea or the imaginary. In painting, the emphasis is on the complete, the fundamental or essential, as opposed to merely the apparent.

RECESSION. A sense of movement or thrust back into the three-dimensional depth of the picture, which, in a balanced composition, is equalized by a return to the two-dimensional picture surface.

RECTIFIED TURPENTINE. See *Turpentine.*

RECTO (L.) In the case of paintings on both sides of a canvas, or drawings on both sides of a paper, etc., the front or original side is considered the *recto* (the obverse) as opposed to the *verso* (the reverse) or back.

RED LEAD. (Minium.) A heavy opaque red made of oxides of lead. No longer used as an artist's color, it is valuable in industry.

REFLECTION, LIGHT. The reflection of light is of two types: diffuse reflection, or spread-out; and specular re-

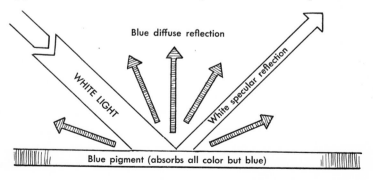

A diagram showing light reflection.

flection, or mirrorlike. When white light strikes an object with a rough surface painted blue, for instance, the rays of the reflected color blue are sent back in all directions (the light of the other colors being absorbed). This is diffuse reflection. If, however, the surface of the object is smooth, there will be the diffuse reflection of the blue color, plus the specular reflection of white light, whose angle of reflection will equal its angle of incidence.

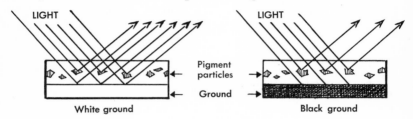

Diagrams showing light reflection.

Practically speaking, a white surface reflects all the rays of light, and a black surface none (although a shiny black surface will have specular reflections). Thus, oil paint over a white ground has more luminosity than that over a black ground. Picture varnish, while giving depth to the color and uniformity to the surface of a painting, can also, when used in excess, produce annoying specular reflections. See also *Color.*

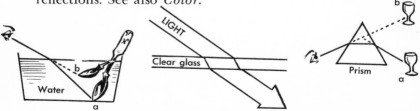

Due to the refraction of light, the actual object at "a" appears at "b."

REFRACTION, LIGHT. The refraction of light is the bending of a light ray as it leaves one medium, such as air, and obliquely enters a denser medium, such as water or a glass prism.

REGIONAL EXHIBITION. See *Exhibition.*

RELINING. When a painting has disintegrated because of age or damage, it may be necessary to mount it on another new backing or support. This process is called "relining" the painting. Linen canvas is generally used, and the adhesive may be either aqueous or non-aqueous glue. If the damage is extreme, it may be necessary to remove the paint layer from the ground, or the paint and ground from the support. This process, with remounting, is called "transferring," and is a more delicate and complex operation. It is used with canvas or panel supports, especially in the restoration of murals. See also *Restoration.*

RENAISSANCE PAINTING. Characterized by a reawakening of the arts and a rebirth in the spirit of the Classical models, the Renaissance was the beginning of modern man's interest in himself as a rationalistic individual. The quality of the Renaissance can be expressed by the term "humanism" or man as the center of the universe, even though the religious subject matter was still used. The Early Renaissance of the 15th century in Italy might be epitomized by the painter Masaccio (1401–1428), whose everyday models were presented in sculptural form, placed in space, and Piero della Francesca (c. 1415–1492), a painter of statuesque figures organized in an interlaced geometrical pattern. During this period, the center was Florence. In the High Renaissance, which was centered in Rome and included Venice and Milan, the characteristic painters could be Leonardo da Vinci (1452–1519), Michaelangelo (1475–1564), and Raphael (1483–1520). Renaissance painting, with its serenity, grandeur, and balanced order, led into Mannerism and then finally to the Baroque in the 17th century. In northern Europe, the Renaissance painters would include such men as Dürer (1471–1528) and Holbein (1498–1543). One outstanding characteristic of the Renaissance in the field of painting was the development of an interest in the pure problems of form, space, color, etc.

RENDERING. The term refers to the techniques involved in the completion of a drawing: refining, adding detail, embellishing, modeling, etc. It implies the realization or achievement of "finish."

REPAINTING. See *Inpainting.*

REPETITION. Refers to the repeating of similar elements in different parts or areas of the painting. Repetition of color creates tensions as the eye relates the same or similar hues. Repetition of line creates vibration and movement, even if the line is used only as a spontaneous reinforcement of volume. Repetition of shape may also occur. In all cases, repetition appears in patterns and textures, and while setting up rhythms, it creates unity in a composition.

REPLICA. A copy of a painting, or other work of art, made by the artist himself and produced without any intention to defraud. See also *Copy.*

REPOUSSOIR (reh-poo-SWAHR). (Fr.) A figure or an object placed in either lower corner or side of the picture (the extreme foreground) for the purpose of directing the viewer's eye into the center or depth of the picture.

REPRESENTATIONAL. In painting, characterized by subject matter of recognizable figures, objects, natural forms, etc., as opposed to non-representional, non-figurative, or abstract.

REPRODUCTION. A copy of a painting, or any work of art, made at a later date by someone other than the original artist. Unlike a forgery, the reproduction is made with honest intent and for legitimate reasons. (It is possible, however, that subsequently it might be used by someone else for fraudulent purposes.) The term also refers to a mechanically printed photoengraving, either in black and white or in color. See also *Facsimile*.

RESIN. Dissolved in a solvent, resins are used separately as varnishes or mixed in paints. They are *natural* or *synthetic*. The natural resins are gums, exuded from trees, which harden on exposure to air. They are also the fossil product from dead trees and are dug from the earth. The synthetic resins, which have been used by artists only relatively recently, are compounds manufactured from coal or petroleum.

Natural resins. Divided into two groups on the basis of their solubility or natural form:
1. The so-called *soft resins:*
   (a) Dammar resin: From a southeast Asian tree. Dissolves in turpentine to make a varnish that is hard and flexible and that yellows only slightly. In permanent painting, it is the most satisfactory of the resins.
   (b) Mastic resin: From a Mediterranean tree. Dissolves in turpentine to make a softer and more yellowing varnish.
   (c) Sandarac resin: From a North African tree. Used in early times, but has been replaced by dammar and mastic.
   (d) Shellac: A colored resin, made from the secretion of an East Indian insect. Dissolves in alcohol. Dries very quickly to form a hard film. Turns dark with age.
2. The so-called *hard resins:*
   (a) Amber: A fossil resin, very hard and clear. No longer readily obtainable, it formerly was used in a cooked oil-resin varnish.
   (b) Copal resin: Originally obtained from fossil resins but now also from varied other sources. It is melted and cooked with linseed oil and added driers, then thinned with volatile solvents to form the most familiar

163

oil-resin type of varnish. It forms an extremely hard film, very resistant to thinners.

Synthetic resins. Of three main types:
1. Acrylic resins: In solutions in acetone, toluene, and turpentine, they serve as fixatives, picture varnishes, and paint thinners. In water emulsions, as binders for prepared gesso and tempera paints.
2. Alkyd resins: In solutions in turpentine, used mainly as industrial paint vehicles or oil paint mediums.
3. Vinyl resins: In solutions in acetone, toluene, and alcohols. Solutions of polyvinyl acetate (p.v.a.) are used as picture varnishes. Water emulsions are used as adhesives and glues, and as binders in tempera paints.

See *Synthetic Resin Paint* and *Varnish*.

RESOLVE. To analyze and sharpen up to a solution a troublesome or inharmonious area of the painting.

RESTORATION. Modern authorities take the view that the restoration of paintings refers only to the replacement of missing parts. Effort is made to retain all possible original paint. In repainting, nothing relative to the pictorial content is added as conjectural elements to put the painting into its supposed original state. Actual damage, however, as it is in itself a change from the original state, is repaired. In extensive restoring with necessary repainting, it should be readily apparent to the viewer where the genuine original work ends and later completion begins.

RESTRICTED PALETTE. The term is used to indicate the considerable limitation by the artist on the number of colors he uses. Limitations may manifest themselves in different ways. For instance, the painter may limit himself to three pigments as close as possible to the three primary hues; he may use variations of only one or two hues, or perhaps of only colors of subdued intensity, etc. In any case, he depends on the minimum sufficient for his purposes. Generally speaking, an average number of colors is fourteen. Thus, a list of four or five, for instance, would be considered a simplified, limited, or restricted palette.

RETARDER. An essential oil added to the painting medium in minute quantities to reduce the drying rate of the paint in order to allow reworking. Actually there is little use of retarders as the introduction of poppyseed oil has the same effect and is safer. Oil of cloves, oil of spike, and oil of lavender are the best known retarders.

RETOUCHING. See *Repainting.*

RETOUCH VARNISH. See *Varnish.*

RETROSPECTIVE. Applied to an exhibition of an individual artist's work, the term indicates a review of that produced throughout his life, rather than only the current or recent work or that of a limited period.

RHYTHM. One of the interrelating principles of design. Rhythm is the repetitive accent in movement occurring at

An example of the use of rhythm. (FROM FRA ANGELICO)

certain intervals. A periodic recurring of the elements of color, line, or shape can help to organize and unify a composition. Progression occurs in rhythm when the interval between accents or elements increases or decreases.

RHYTHMIC. Having the properties of rhythm. See *Rhythm*.

ROCOCO. The chief European style of decoration of the 18th century. As a reaction against the heavier Baroque style of the reign of Louis XIV in France, it was charming, graceful, and of studied artificiality. Characterized by curvilinear, asymmetrical ornamentation with S-curves, shell forms, etc., it was a style of courtly pleasure. Its characteristics are exemplified in Italy by the work of the painter Tiepolo (1696–1770); in France, by Watteau (1684–1721), Boucher (1703–1770), and Fragonard (1732–1806). In England, Hogarth (1697–1764) is considered to have been influenced by the Rococo. As an architectural style, it reached a climax in Germany and Austria. A reaction to the Rococo took place in the Neo-Classicism of the latter part of the 18th century.

ROLLER. The house painter's paint roller is occasionally employed by contemporary artists to cover large areas and to obtain a certain textural effect or surface quality, depending upon the type of cylinder used.

ROMANESQUE. See *Medieval Painting*.

ROMAN PAINTING. Unlike the painting of the Greek period, a considerable amount of Roman painting has survived. This is in palaces and villas, principally at Pompeii, where examples date back to c. 100 B.C. The Roman painters made an effort to solve problems of visual illusion. With the figures and objects in a spatial environment there is a modeling of form with light and dark and a use of foreshortening. Some of the sketchiness and loose-

166

ness of the background gives additional depth through aerial perspective. With all this effort at the tangible and realistic, there is a loss of some of the charm and grace of earlier periods of decoration. The paintings in Pompeii are true fresco. The plaster was very thick, being a mixture of marble dust. Brilliant colors, reds, and blacks enliven the effect, which has a polished sheen. In the late Roman Empire, there was an increase of more abstract concepts in an attempt to express something more than the literal and the visual.

ROMANTICISM. A reaction against the conservative Neo-Classicism, the Romantic movement expressed the emotional revival of Renaissance individualism. A poetic imagination and a passionate concern with "feeling" were characteristics of painters associated with Romanticism, which lasted until the middle of the 19th century. In France, Géricault (1791–1824) was the first real leader of the movement, followed by Delacroix (1798–1863), its major painter; the latter typified the struggling nonconforming artist who battles the established Academy. With dramatic and exotic subject matter, Delacroix developed emotional color, handled freely in Baroque compositions. Other works of influence in the Romantic movement were the objective landscapes of Constable (1776–1837) in England and the powerful satirical work of Goya (1746–1828) in Spain.

ROSIN. The material used on violin bows and boxers' soles is rosin, a type of resin. It is the residue from the distillation of turpentine. Although sometimes found in inferior or cheaper industrial paints, it is not used in permanent painting.

RUBBING. A method of obtaining a texture or image by placing a thin material, usually damp paper, over a raised or indented surface and then rubbing the uneven surface of the paper with a flat chalk, pencil, or pad of ink or paint. The rubbings of archaeological reliefs and old tombstones are examples. Use has been made of rubbings (called *frottage*) of textures such as wood grain, weave patterns, etc., to supply material for *collage*.

S

SAFFLOWER OIL. A drying oil that is made from the seeds of the safflower plant and is used as a binding medium in oil painting. It has been ground with white paints and is reputed to compare favorably with linseed oil, yellowing less.

SALON D'AUTOMNE (sah-LOH*n* doh-TAWN). (Fr.) A yearly autumn exhibition in Paris, founded in 1903 with Bonnard, Marquet, Matisse, and others. Notable for the first showing, in 1905, of the Fauves and for the great memorial exhibition of Cézanne in 1907.

SALON DES INDÉPENDANTS (sah-LOH*n* day-zan-day-pahn-DAH*n*). (Fr.) An exhibition first organized in 1884 by a group of independent French painters whose work had been rejected at the official Salon. The group, which refused to subscribe to the worn-out views of the École des Beaux-Arts, then formed a permanent society called Société des Artistes Indépendants in order to organize jury-free yearly spring exhibitions. Originally including such painters as Cross, Guillaumin, Redon, Seurat, and Signac, the organization later exhibited additional members, among them Bonnard, van Gogh, (Henri) Rousseau, and Lautrec.

SALON DES REFUSÉS (sah-LOH*n* day ruh-fiu-ZAY.) (Fr.)

In 19th-century Paris the official biennial exhibitions, or Salons, came so much under the control of the ultraconservative Academy of Fine Arts that protests were raised. The protests became so strong and the number of painters rejected became so numerous (over 4000) that, in 1863, Napoleon III ordered a special exhibition—the only one of its kind. This was the Salon des Refusés, or the Salon of the Rejected. It is sometimes used as one of the starting dates for so-called Modern Art. Among the painters who exhibited were Manet, Cézanne, Pissarro, Boudin, Fantin-Latour, and Whistler.

SANDARAC. See *Resin*.

SANGUINE. Not a pigment, but a name for a color—a brownish blood-red.

SATURATION. See *Color*.

SCALE. The whole consideration of the relative enlarging or reducing of size, whether to adjust to scientific perspective, according to psychological interests, or for aesthetic reasons; in reference particularly to human proportions.

SCALING. The term, applied to a paint layer, means flaking paint; in addition, the process of enlarging and reducing. See also *Scale*.

SCARLET. The name sometimes given to a red somewhere between crimson and the primary red hue of light. See *Color* and *Color Wheel*.

SCARLET LAKE. Brilliant orange-red pigment now made as a lake from aniline dyestuffs. Not permanent.

SCHEMA (SKEE-muh). (L.) The plan or design; the format.

SCHEMATIC. A term referring to systematic planning, with logical steps to a conclusion. Sometimes used to indicate an emphasis on the structural plan of the picture at the expense of richness of content.

SCHOOL. An all-inclusive word having several meanings. (1) The simplest is that associated with an individual, e.g., School of Rubens. This means work done by his apprentices or assistants, or in his style by followers with lesser genius. (2) There is the geographical association of a certain place, for instance: with a country, as Italian School; a city, School of Paris; or an area, Hudson River School. (3) A similar outlook will enable painters to be grouped together, as the painters of the Ashcan School, for example. In most cases, of course, the shorter the time encompassed, the more defined the "school" can be.

SCHWEINFURT GREEN. See *Emerald Green.*

SCRUFFING. A term sometimes used to describe scumbling with an extremely "short" and stiff paint, in which the texture of the underlayer gives the broken effect. It is also referred to as "dragging." See *Scumbling.*

SCUMBLING. A term used to describe the uneven application of an opaque or a semi-opaque layer of paint over a dried underlayer. Scumbling is often of a lighter value than the paint it partially covers. It differs from the transparent glaze that alters but still allows the entire underlayer to remain visible. See also *Glaze.*

SECCO. Italian word for "dry." See *Fresco.*

SECONDARY COLORS. See *Color Wheel.*

SECTION D'OR, La (lah sehk-SYOH*n* DOHR). (Fr.) A group of Cubist painters who exhibited in Paris in 1912 under that name (The Golden Section). The exhibition was organized as a tribute to Cézanne. The term is derived from the name given to a proportional division. See *Golden Section.*

SEICENTO (say-ee-CHEN-toh). (It.) The 1600's, or the 17th century.

SENSITIZED CANVAS. Canvas prepared with a chemical coating that retains any image, such as a photograph or drawing projected thereon. Occasionally used by illustrators and some contemporary painters.

SEPIA. A powerful, dark brown transparent color made from the ink bag of the cuttlefish or squid. Used only in inks and water colors, and not always permanent.

SERIGRAPHY. Printing in the fine arts by the silk-screen process. Used by some contemporary "painters."

SEZESSIONISTS. See *Art Nouveau.*

SFUMATO (sfoo-MAH-toh). (It.) Describes the blending of tones of color or value by smooth and indistinguishable gradations; forms blended with soft smokelike contours into the darkness of a shadowed background.

SGRAFFITO (sgrah-FEE-toh). (It.) (Also *Graffito.*) The technique (originating in fresco and ceramic work) of producing lines by scratching through a glaze or paint layer to reveal a different colored ground beneath. Usually done with the handle of the brush.

SHADE. (1) The term refers to the absence of light, as in light and shade. To "shade" a drawing is to manipulate tones of gray, adding gradations of value from light to dark; to model it. See *Modeling.* (2) A shade of a particular color is the hue altered and darkened with the addition of black, or neutralized with the addition of a complementary color. See also *Color.*

SHADING. The areas of tone, usually in a drawing, that model the form. See *Modeling.*

171

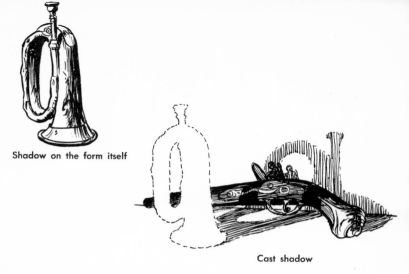

Shadow on the form itself

Cast shadow

Different types of shadow.

SHADOW. Shade within certain defined limits, in contrast to light or lighted areas. Shadow can be one of two types: (1) on the form itself, created by the structure of the form, and (2) created by the form and projected onto another form or plane, in which case it is called a *cast shadow*. See also *Chiaroscuro* and *Shade.*

SHAPE. Although the term is used interchangeably with form, in painting shape implies a two-dimensional area enclosed by an outline (while form is three-dimensional— a mass or volume). In the figure-ground relationship, shapes are either positive (the figure) or negative (the ground). The outline of a shape may be linear and hard-edged or soft and indistinct. Shapes have relative size, dark and light value, texture, and directional movement. The position or orientation of a shape governs how it is seen, and (as Professor Rudolf Arnheim has emphasized) in case of any ambiguity, shapes will tend to be interpreted in their simplest configuration. See *Form, Plane,* and *Space.*

172

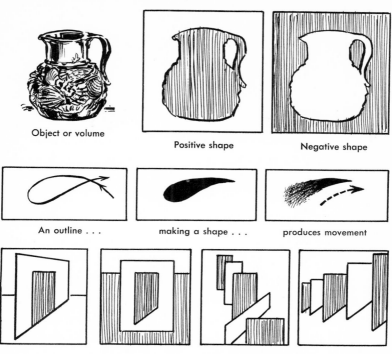

Object or volume

Positive shape

Negative shape

An outline . . .

making a shape . . .

produces movement

Different aspects of the same two-dimensional shape

Examples of shape.

SHAPED CANVAS. Canvas stretched over a frame of wood or metal in any shape other than that of the traditional two-dimensional painting: the rectangular, the oval, or the round. When the canvas is constructed in three dimensions, the viewer responds to it as sculptural form. Often free standing, these forms have little to do with the pictorial qualities of painting.

SHELLAC. A colored resin, made from the secretion of insects in India. Soluble in alcohol, but not turpentine or mineral spirits, it is used mainly as size for wall painting, gesso, and gilding, and sometimes for a fixative. It is unsatisfactory as a varnish in permanent painting even though it forms a hard flexible film, for it turns dark with age.

173

SHORT PAINT. Paint that is stiff (non-flowing or "crisp") and in which brush marks will be retained. See also *Long Paint*.

SHOW. An exhibition. See *Exhibition*.

SICCATIF DE COURTRAI. See *Drier*.

SICCATIF DE HAARLEM. See *Drier*.

SICCATIVE. A drier. See *Drier*.

SIENNA. See *Raw Sienna* and *Burnt Sienna*.

SILHOUETTE. The representation of an object so presented that it is a shape in profile and a flat uniform tone in color.

SILICON-ESTER PAINTING. A relatively recent development on water-glass painting, in which the pigments are bound in a silica, usually ethyl silicate. It appears to be adaptable to mural painting.

SIMULTANEISM. A later form of Orphism. See *Orphic Cubism*.

SIMULTANEITY. Describes an object in various aspects, or seen from various points of view, at the same moment. *Simultaneism* is a word given to these superimposed images presented in the same painting. It was used extensively by the Cubists and Futurists.

SIMULTANEOUS CONTRAST. The principle that colors are modified in their appearance when juxtaposed in proximity to one another. Their modification is greatest at their point, or edge, of contact. This change is due to a human tendency to increase the contrast between colors while evaluating it. The eye seems to require the complementary hue for any given color and will create it when it is not actually present. Several laws of Simultaneous

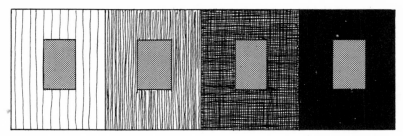

The edges of the large squares appear to be modified in value where they meet. The small squares appear to change value as their backgrounds change.

Example of simultaneous contrast.

Contrast were formulated in 1839 by the French chemist M. E. Chevreul. See also *Contrast*.

SIZE. Various gluey materials used to fill in the pores of paper or the weave of canvas and to isolate different layers. Size is used, for example, to protect the fabric of canvas from the rotting effect of an oil ground laid over it. See *Glue*.

SKETCH. A preparatory drawing or painting done for a subsequent more intensively treated and often larger final version. Also refers to work done quickly and usually from the *motif*. To "sketch" or to "make a sketch," therefore, is to turn out a quick interpretation or a rapid notation.

SKETCHING EASEL. A light portable collapsible tripod used to hold the painting when working from the *motif*. Some sketching easels are combined with the sketch box in one compact unit.

SKIN GLUE. See *Glue*.

SLAB. A heavy piece of plate glass (sometimes white), porcelain, or marble used in grinding paints with a muller.

SLICK. A term applied to an overelaborated perfection of superficial surface quality and the development of form and detail to an excessive degree, weakening any expressive quality the painting might have.

SMALT. Formerly, an impermanent blue associated with ceramic glazes; now replaced by cobalt blue or ultramarine blue.

SOCIAL REALISM. A term generally applied to any socially conscious representational painting, but specifically to that of the 1930's in the United States. Dealing with such themes as unemployment, poverty, and class warfare, it was often politically propagandist in nature.

SOCIÉTÉ DES ARTISTES INDÉPENDANTS. (so-see-ay-TAY day-zahr-TEEST-zan-day-pahn-DAHn). See *Salon des Indépendants*.

SOCIÉTÉ DES VINGT (so-see-ay-TAY day VAn). (Fr.) Society of the Twenty. See *Vingt, Les*.

SOI-DISANT (swah-dee-ZAHn). (Fr.) Self-styled, as a so-called or would-be artist.

SOLID. Having three-dimensional mass or volume. See *Volume*.

SOLVENT. A liquid that is capable of dissolving certain solids and putting them into solution. A mutual solvent is capable of being mixed with two different materials that normally would not be compatible. The powerful, volatile solvents, some of which are very poisonous and highly flammable, and which should be used with care, are: benzine, benzene, toluene, various alcohols, and acetone.

SOYA BEAN OIL. As a substitute for linseed oil, the bleached oil of soya beans is used in industrial paints and varnishes. As an artist's oil, it is a poor drier and is inferior to linseed oil.

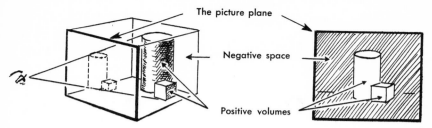

The picture plane

Negative space

Positive volumes

Diagrams showing the relationship of
three-dimensional space to the picture plane.

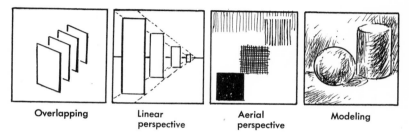

| Overlapping | Linear perspective | Aerial perspective | Modeling |

Several methods of creating space.

SPACE.   The unoccupied area of a painting, within which
certain activities, certain tensions exist. Although the term
"positive space" is sometimes used for objects, they could
be better described as positive shapes or positive volumes
in contrast to space or negative space. Space exists two-
dimensionally on the picture plane or canvas surface and
(as an illusion) three-dimensionally in the depth of the
picture box. The relationship of these two different concepts of space is essential to modern painting. The organization of planes, volumes, or objects in space is naturally
of prime importance to the painter. The manner of
creating space, filling it, and making it aesthetically meaningful is his problem. He uses such manipulations as the
overlapping of planes and forms, linear and aerial perspective, open and closed contours, contrasts of color,
value, and shape, and the control of tensions and move-

ments to make the illusion and the reality of space a contributing factor in his total expression. See *Shape* and *Volume*.

SPACE ARTS.   See *Plastic Arts.*

SPACE TIME.   A concept taken from physics, and related to art criticism, which maintains that time and space are inseparable. Beyond the basic premise that nothing can exist without being in time (the fourth dimension), there is an active relationship between space and time in every painting. In two-dimensional space (of height and width), size or distance can set the time period in the stroke of the artist's brush through space across the surface of the canvas. Time also, then, is involved in the viewer's experience as he later sees and follows the image of the stroke. Time, as it elapses while the viewer's eye moves over the surface of the painting, is thus a part of his appreciation. A more complex relationship with time exists with the addition of the third dimension in the illusionary spatial depth of the painting. The varied intervals of time make different rhythms and accents throughout the composition as the viewer's attention moves through the depicted space. See also *Space*.

SPANISH RED.   A bluish-red of native iron oxide. It is grouped with the so-called "earth colors."

SPECTRUM.   See *Color* and *Light*.

SPECULAR REFLECTION.   See *Reflection, Light*.

SPIKE, OIL OF.   A drying retarder. See *Retarder*.

SPIRIT VARNISH.   A natural resin dissolved in a solvent as opposed to a cooked oil-resin varnish. See *Varnish*.

SPLIT COMPLEMENTARY.   See *Color Wheel*.

SPONTANEITY.   The quality of impulse, of automatic

178

response or emotional directness much prized in the techniques of certain contemporary schools of painting—sometimes to the exclusion of any other quality.

SPONTANEOUS COMBUSTION. The self-igniting and bursting into flame of oily paint rags caused by the oxidation of the drying oils spread over an extended surface and the heat build-up in the folds of the cloth. In the studio, this potentially dangerous situation can exist if oil-soaked rags are allowed to pile up in closets or flammable containers.

SPRAY GUN. An electrically driven device used to apply varnishes, paints, etc., the best of which deliver a constant, well-atomized, fan-shaped spray. These also have a trap to prevent condensed moisture or dirt from mixing into the liquid sprayed.

SPRAY PRESSURE CAN. Various varnishes, fixatives, and paints are available in cans with a neutral gas under pressure. These furnish a simple and quick spray application, but products vary and are sometimes of unreliable quality. A device using a can of replaceable propellant gas that can be employed with the artist's own choice of liquid is also obtainable.

SQUARE-OFF. (Also Square-Up.) A method of enlarging (or reducing) or simply transferring a drawing by means

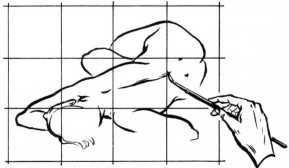
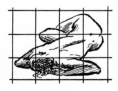

Enlarging by using superimposed squares.

of a superimposed network of lines forming squares. (The greater the number of squares, the more accurate the process.) The original drawing is covered with a set of squares; each square in the second set (on the wall or canvas) is filled, using the first set as a guide.

STABILIZERS. Various materials added to paints to keep the pigment and oil from separating in the tube and to give proper brushing consistency. They can be waxes, aqueous solutions, or other inert additives.

STAIN. See *Pigments*.

STAND OIL. See *Linseed Oil*.

STAPLE. The familiar small bent wire in a square "U" shape, which is driven by a spring staple gun. Staples are used instead of tacks to fasten stretched canvas to the stretcher strips. Their advantage over tacks seems only in speed as they do not hold as well, rust more easily, and are more difficult to remove.

STATIC. Describes any elment of a painting that is passive, without motion or activity, as contrasted with those elements that are active, dynamic, and influential.

STENCIL. A mechanical aid in applying an area of paint repetitiously. The stencil, made of metal, cardboard, or heavy paper or plastic is cut out in such a way as to allow paint to be brushed or sprayed through the open areas. Letters and numbers are available in stencil form and have been used by contemporary painters.

STEREOCHROMY. See *Water-Glass Painting*.

STIJL, De (duh STYLE). (Dutch) The Style. Originating as a magazine in Leyden, Holland, in 1917, *de Stijl* was the name given the attempt by a group of painters (including Mondrian), architects, and designers to apply principles of geometric abstraction to the fine and applied arts. Its later ideas were incorporated into the principles advocated in the Bauhaus in Germany.

STILL LIFE. A picture having inanimate objects as its subject matter. Before the 16th century, the still life was to be found only as detail in larger compositions, usually of religious subjects. The first form to emerge was the symbolic collection of objects, such as the skull and the hourglass, used as reminders of death and the transience of life. These are known as *Memento Mori* (L., "Remember that you must die") and *Vanitas* (L., "Vanity, emptiness"). Gradually, the religious symbols of bread, wine, and water appeared, and the still life developed to include flowers, a display of food (often opulent), and objects of the hunt.

STIMMUNG (SHTIM-oong). (Ger.) The general mood.

STIPPLE. A method of obtaining a tone by drawing many small dots.

STOMP (or *Stump*). A tight roll of soft gray paper pointed at each end and about the size of a large cigar. It is used to rub charcoal, chalk, and pastel to obtain smooth areas or transitions of tone. A smaller roll, the size of a thin pencil and pointed only at one end, is called a *tortillon*.

STRASBOURG TURPENTINE. See *Oleoresin*.

STRETCHER. Stretcher bars or strips make up the wood frame on which canvas is stretched to form a painting support. In the 18th century, the present system of slotted corners was developed. Keys or small wedges are provided which, when driven into the slots, enlarge the frame and tighten the canvas. The usual stretcher strips are manufactured $1\frac{3}{4}'' \times \frac{3}{4}''$ in thickness. A stretcher of about 36 inches or over in length is cross-braced. Heavier stretcher strips ($2\frac{1}{2}'' \times 1\frac{1}{8}''$) can be purchased, as well as custom-built sizes with furniture expansion joints in the corners.

In length, stretcher strips are available in every inch size up to 36 inches, after which they are made in even sizes only. See also *Stretching Canvas.*

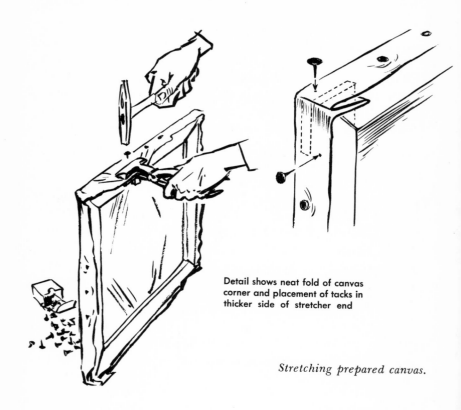

Detail shows neat fold of canvas corner and placement of tacks in thicker side of stretcher end

Stretching prepared canvas.

STRETCHING CANVAS. The process of fastening canvas to a frame of stretcher bars. If unprepared canvas is used, it is not actually stretched over the frame but fastened rather loosely, as the application of glue size will tighten it. In the process, the canvas is laid horizontally on a flat surface with the frame on top. Alternate sides are folded up and tacked, one tack at a time. If prepared canvas is used, actual stretching is necessary, and stretching pliers may be used, with the canvas held vertically; a magnetic tack hammer facilitates the operation. In place of hammer and tacks, a staple gun using half-inch staples is often used.

STRIKE THROUGH. See *Bleeding*.

STRIPPING. Quick and economical framing is often done with simple strip molding of $1\frac{1}{2}'' \times \frac{5}{16}''$ nailed around the painting directly onto the stretcher bars. Stripping may be edged with gold or silver leaf, plastic, or metal.

STRONTIUM YELLOW. A pale cool yellow made of strontium chromate. Permanent.

STUDIO. (French: *atelier.*) The workshop of a painter. Studios range from the single spare room or back shed to elaborate quarters with high ceilings, north light, and living facilities. The high ceiling reduces reflections and allows space for large canvases; the north light gives a constant illumination from the sky without the changing position of the sun. Studios of many urban artists are factory lofts.

STUDY. A study is a section or detail of a painting or drawing made to solve difficulties that might arise later in the final version.

STUMP. See *Stomp*.

STURM, Der (dair SHTOORM.) (Ger.) The name of a magazine, founded in Berlin in 1910, that began to publish the work of Expressionists. In 1912, it was associated with a gallery that exhibited the work of *Die Brüke* and *Der Blaue Reiter*.

STYLE. Those common characteristics that relate the paintings of an historical period, a cultural heritage, or a racial or national environment. These characteristics are of manner and form, not of content. An individual artist's personal style is his unique approach to life, his attitude toward it and toward his painting. It is evidenced in such things as his characteristic paint handling, brushwork, drawing, color, and subject matter. True style cannot be assumed, but it can be modified with conscious intent and effort.

STYLE, The. See *Stijl, De.*

SUBJECTIVE. Pertaining to the emphasis on the interior qualities of the artist's mind, his experience, knowledge, etc. In painting, this is associated with the conceptual approach as opposed to the objective and perceptual. See *Conceptual Painting.*

SUBJECT MATTER. The term is used in referring to the visual recognizable subject—or object—that exists as the artist's point of departure for his painting. There are several traditional types, some existing in combination, which can be grouped as follows:

Cityscapes. Urban views, street scenes, industrial scenes.
Figures. Costumed, draped, or dressed humans; nudes.
Genre. Scenes of figures in typical activities of everyday life.
Interiors. Scenes in rooms or enclosed spaces, etc., with or without figures.
Landscapes. Views of a certain amount of terrain at any distance.
Marines. Seascapes, views of the sea, or the edge of the sea, etc.
Portraits. Likenesses of actual individuals; heads, three-quarter, or entire figures.
Still life. Fruit, flowers, food, and other objects.

In much contemporary painting, the paint itself and how

it has been manipulated can be the subject matter. The relationships of colors, shapes, lines, tensions, movements, etc., may suffice for certain painters, while others may want the additional psychological and emotional factors that can be obtained through the relationship of a visual recognizable subject. In any case, the content or meaning of a painting is not to be found in the subject matter, but in the painting of it.

SUBTRACTIVE COLOR MIXTURE. See *Color.*

SUCCÈS DE SCANDALE (sook-SAY duh skah*n*-DAL). (Fr.) A success by virtue of public outrage.

SUCCÈS D'ESTIME (sook-SAY deh-STEEM). (Fr.) A success critically, but not popularly.

SUN-THICKENED OIL. See *Linseed Oil.*

SUPPORT. The basic material upon which the painting is created—be it canvas, wood, cardboard, wallboard, metal, etc.—is called the support.

SUPREMATISM. A purely abstract geometric form of Cubism founded about 1913 by Malevich (1878–1935).

SURFACE COLOR. See *Color.*

SURREALISM. A broad movement in literature and art that existed between the two World Wars. It was named by the eccentric French poet Apollinaire and officially founded by the poet-painter Breton who, in his "Surrealist Manifesto" of 1924, stated the intentions of the movement. These included the effort to remove rationality from the creative process and to replace it with subconscious manifestations, especially those expounded by Freud. The belief in the superior reality of associations, the supremacy of the subconscious impulse, and the "omnipotence of the dream" were basic as a way of looking at life. Surrealism, which combined the nihilism of Dada with many abstract aspects of Cubism and Futurism, developed in two general styles; the one, using meticulous, traditional techniques to illustrate the visions and dreams; and the other, a non-figurative, more spontaneous, and impulsive style called *Abstract Surrealism*. The anti-aesthetic attitudes of Dada have, through Surrealism, re-emerged in Pop Art, Action Painting, Psychedelic Art, and the Environments of the contemporary "art" scene, as well as in the literature of Happenings, the Beat poets, and the Theater of the Absurd. See also *Dada*.

SYMBOL. A symbol in painting is an abstracted visual intermediary used to communicate a universal idea or complex meaning remote in space and time, the significance of which is other than the aesthetic quality of the symbol itself. Signs are more explicit than symbols as they are of the tangible factual world and, being conventionally precise, exist as signals. Symbols function actively in a more emotional world of meaning through imagery. Most result from established usage and association, though many are personal to the painter and, as such, sometimes difficult to decipher. In a sense, a representational painting itself can be considered a symbol, because it can never be the object it depicts. Much contemporary painting attempts to reconcile this dichotomy.

SYMBOLISM. A method used in art of revealing or suggesting intangible ideas or emotional truths by use of signs or symbols. The term was also used as the name for a French literary movement to which a group of painters were allied, calling themselves *Synthetists* and *Symbolists*. See *Symbol* and *Synthetism*.

SYNCHROMISM. A colorful and geometrically abstract development of Post-Impressionism and Cubism; founded in Paris in 1913 and brought to America by S. MacDonald-Wright and Morgan Russell.

SYNTHETIC CUBISM. See *Cubism.*

SYNTHETIC RESIN. See *Resin.*

SYNTHETIC RESIN PAINT. Although used since the 1930's in paints for industry, synthetic resins have been extensively used by the artist only since the 1950's. There are four basic types of synthetic resin paints as follows (with examples):

Acrylics. Methyl methacrylate resin supplied in water emulsions; "Liquitex" ("Rhoplex"), "New-Temp." Two products compatible with linseed oil and turpentine are "Lucite" and "Magna" colors.
Alkyds. In solutions thinned with turpentine, these paints are used mainly in industry.
Copolymers. Mixtures of acrylics and vinyls; "New Masters," thinned with water.
Vinyls. Polyvinyl acetate (p.v.a.) emulsions are thinned with water; "Polymer Tempera."

Latex types of house paint may have either an acrylic resin or a vinyl resin base, or they may consist of a combination of both. They are water-thinned. See also *Resin.*

SYNTHETIC RESIN VARNISH. See *Resin* and *Varnish.*

SYNTHETISM. Also called *Symbolism* or *Cloisonnisme.* A Post-Impressionist movement that centered in Pont-Aven in the late 1880's and attempted, by using strong colors and heavy outlines, to "synthesize" the visible world and to produce paintings that would be "symbolic" or expressive of emotions, ideas, etc. Gauguin (1848–1903) was the most outstanding painter of the movement, which had actually started as a literary one.

T

TACHISME (tah-SHEEZ-mih). (Fr.) A term used to describe a style of painting in which the color is applied in splotches or blots (*taches*) of color. These are placed on the canvas spontaneously and by chance. *Tachisme* has been associated with a group of French painters active since World War II.

TACHISTE. Refers to *Tachisme*. See *Tachisme*.

TACTILE VALUE. The quality in a painting related to the sense of touch. The tactile elements in the paint surface, for instance, even though one does not actually feel them with the fingers, communicate an expressive quality. Also, the term refers to the qualities represented within the painting, such as the surface texture of forms and objects. See also *Paint Quality* and *Texture*.

TALC. Native magnesium silicate sometimes used as a white extender in paint.

TALENT. Innate aptitude for expression. This natural endowment is usually regarded as ability in the facility of expression only, and not in the quality of expression.

TECHNIQUE. The painter's technique is his method of working. See *Mixed Technique, Paint Quality,* and *Underpainting.*

TECTONIC. Structural or architectural. In painting, the word is used to describe those qualities tending toward an equalization between the vertical and the horizontal. It is associated with a somewhat rigid balance in the composition and related to a central axis. Also, that which pertains to a designed construction as opposed to the biomorphic.

TELEOLOGICAL. The characteristic of being shaped by a purpose to an end. Especially applied to the natural process of growth, but also used in the art criticism of paintings and sculpture. The term comes from the philosophical belief that the universe is dominated by a purpose, as opposed to the theory that mechanics can explain organic life.

TEMPERA. A technique of painting using egg yolk thinned with water or with other emulsions as mediums. True tempera paints produce water-resistant films, tough and permanent. (The term should not be applied to the simple water or glue techniques such as gouache or distemper.) In brush handling, because tempera tends to dry very rapidly, thin translucent hatching strokes are usually applied with pointed water-color sables. The support is rigid, either gesso on panel or linen canvas mounted on panel. There are many variations in tempera painting: (1) pure egg yolk with water only; (2) emulsion of egg yolk, water, and an oil varnish medium; (3) a glue of gum arabic in emulsion with heavy, oily ingredients; (4) a combination, as an underpaint, of any of the above with an oil medium over the top as glazes and loose opaques— or, in some cases, an egg/oil mixture is painted wet into a wet oil-medium color; (5) other emulsions of waxy (beeswax) or resinous ingredients. See also *Mixed Technique.*

TENSION. Visual tension is the dynamic relationship between pictorial objects, axes, planes, etc., that is apparent as a gravitational pull or force of attraction. Tension can exist within shapes or forms created by a distortion of their logical or natural contours. See also *Balance.*

TERRA ALBA. White Earth. See *Gypsum.*

TERRA VERTE. A green earth color. See *Green Earth.*

TERTIARY COLORS. See *Color Wheel.*

TESSERAE. (pl.) (L.) Small odd-shaped bits of glass,

stone, and tile used in mosaic. The term has been used to describe a style of paint-handling in broken patches of color. See also *Mosaic*.

TEXTURE. Related primarily to the sense of touch, or tactile values, the term can refer to two different types of surfaces; the actual and the depicted. (1) Texture describes the surface effect of the actual support, such as canvas weave, smooth wood panel, etc., or of the paint application, such as broken color, glazes, heavy brush, or painting knife strokes, etc., or of pigment qualities such as those obtained by the addition of sand, marble dust, etc. (2) Texture also is present in the pictorial elements. It is experienced in the nature of the surfaces of wood, glass, metal, cloth, skin, etc. And detail or elaboration of the depicted elements can sometimes be considered a form of texture. Textural qualities in all instances, of course, are related to aesthetic considerations. See also *Paint Quality*.

Textures from the support surface, etc.

Textures from the pictorial elements.

THALO BLUE. See *Phthalocyanine Blue*.

THEME. A term sometimes used to describe that element that recurs throughout a painting and exists as a means of transmitting its meaning.

THENARD'S BLUE. See *Cobalt Blue*.

THINNER. Thinners are used primarily to reduce the thickness of paints and varnishes, allowing them to be applied to the painting in workable films. Thinners dry by evaporation, leaving little or no trace of themselves, and they have no binding ability. (See *Binders.*) They are also used as solvents; for instance, turpentine is used to dissolve lumps of dammar to make (liquid) varnish as well as to dissolve old varnish in the process of picture cleaning. The usual thinners are water (in water-color painting), turpentine, and mineral spirits. In many studios, especially those of restorers, are found the more powerful volatile solvents, some of which are very poisonous and highly flammable: benzine, benzene, toluene, various alcohols, and acetone.

THIO VIOLET. A brilliant, relatively new lake color made from aniline dyestuff. Considered neither absolutely permanent nor nonbleeding.

THREE-DIMENSIONAL. Existing in more than one plane. Having the three dimensions of height, width, and depth. Three-dimensional volumes exist in three-dimensional space. See also *Space* and *Volume.*

THRUST. Pressure or force, which in a painting is usually derived from mass or volume. Thrust has movement and therefore direction. The term implies a three-dimensional quality.

TIGHT. A carefully delineated and rigidly linear paint handling or drawing. The opposite of loose. See *Loose.*

TIME. See *Space Time.*

TINT. Any variation of a color away from the pure hue and in the direction of lighter value—usually obtained by an addition of white. See also *Color.*

TITANIUM WHITE. A recently developed (1920) pigment made from titanium dioxide. It is nontoxic, is very opaque, and has strong tinting power; but it is a slow drier and does not form as tough or as flexible a paint film as flake white. Used in water techniques.

TOLUENE (Toluol).   A strong solvent, distilled from coal tar. It is less volatile and safer to use than Benzene.

TONAL.   The use, in painting, of different tones, or a range of values. See *Tone* and *Value*.

TONDO (TOHN-doh).   (It.)   This word for "round" is sometimes used in referring to a painting of that shape.

TONE.   An individual gradation in the form of a particular shade or tint of a color, also, more precisely, of a particular value of neutral dark and light. The term is also used in describing the modification of a color as to "tone down" a color, i.e., to reduce its brilliance or contrast.

TONED GROUND.   A ground with a thin application of color glazed over it to provide more pictorial cohesiveness in the picture. This glaze is also called an *imprimatura*. See also *Imprimatura*.

TONERS.   Various types of precipitated aniline dyestuffs used in concentrated form with little or no inert material as a lake base. As colors, they have a tendency to bleed and are generally fugitive.

TOOTH.   A term used to describe the comparative roughness of a surface of dried glue, paint, or varnish. It has a physical effect on how a subsequent layer of paint goes on and how well it adheres.

TORTILLON (tor-tee-YOHn).   (Fr.)   See *Stomp*.

TOUR DE FORCE.   (Fr.)   A notable or unusual feat of skill; an ingenius accomplishment beyond the ordinary.

TOXICITY.   The state, quality, or degree of being poisonous. The painter is often called upon to use materials that are toxic and capable of causing severe complications if handled without regard for certain considerations. First of all, there are the compounds containing lead, such as flake white, Naples yellow, and the lead chromates. If absorbed into the human system by mouth, by breathing, or through cuts in the skin, lead is a cumulative poison. This means toxicity is built up by small, apparently ineffectual amounts. The painter should not handle these pigments in dry form without a mask. Preferably, he should purchase them in paste form, already ground. Hands, with especial care to the fingernails, should be thoroughly cleaned after using these paints. For this purpose the lanolin soaps in tubes and cans are effective. Chronic lead poisoning is well known in history, and the intestinal disturbance with its complications has been labeled "painter's colic." Pigments containing arsenic, such as one form of cobalt violet and emerald green, are best eliminated from the palette. Naturally, pastels and chalks made of any of the above pigments are to be avoided, as the dust can be inhaled or otherwise easily taken into the system. Obviously, the tendency to moisten the tip of the brush with the mouth, while using the water-color techniques, is a dangerous habit. Lastly, the fumes of such solvents as benene (benzol) and methyl alcohol (methanol, wood alcohol) are highly poisonous. Even the fumes of carbon tetrachloride are dangerous without proper ventilation.

TRADITIONAL. An inclusive term that refers to the type of painting that conforms to the basic disciplines handed down from the past and reflects certain inherited cultural attitudes. Even though a style of painting may have originated in a protest against tradition, over a period of time it can become a part of tradition. This is because it has proven to be in essence more than mere protest. "Traditional painting" is thus a relative term, but, fundamentally, it excludes any current fashionable style that does not appear to concern itself with the values and ideals of the past. See also *Academic* and *Avant-Garde.*

TRANSFERRING. See *Relining.*

TRANSLUCENCY. The quality of a glaze, or a layer of paint considerably thinned with oil or varnish to allow an under coat of paint to show partly through. With age, such a layer mixed with linseed oil will increase its translucency, becoming nearly transparent. See *Pentimento.*

TRICKLING. The repelling by a glazed surface of an additional coating of paint or varnish. This can occur as well when the first surface contains an excess of oil.

TRIPTYCH. (TRIP-tik). (Gr.) A painting in three parts. Usually, the religious triptych or altarpiece has the Madonna and Child or the Crucifixion on the center panel, which is twice as wide as the side wings. The side wings are often hinged to fold over the center as protection. Also, Japanese wood-block prints have been often designed as a single composition spread over three parts.

TROMPE L'OEIL (trohnp LUHY). (Fr.) Literally, to deceive the eye—into believing that the painted object is real. See also *Illusionism.*

TURPENTINE (Turps). The most popular thinner for thinning paints and solvent for making varnish. It is colorless, with a nontoxic vapor and an agreeable odor. Turpentine is distilled from the gum or sap of pine trees and is sometimes called "spirits of turpentine" or "oil of turpentine." The painter uses only the "Pure Gum Spirits of Turpentine," sold in bulk and regulated by the government to be pure and free from water, or the more expensive double distilled or "Rectified Turpentine," sold in art stores in small containers.

TURQUOISE. The greenish-blue color that is close to the primary blue hue of the color wheel based on three primary paint hues. See also *Color Wheel.*

TWENTY, The. See *Vingt, Les.*

TWO-DIMENSIONAL. Flat or existing in one plane, and considered to have only the two dimensions of height and width. Two-dimensional shapes exist in two-dimensional space. See also *Plane* and *Space.*

U

ULTRAMARINE. The genuine pigment has been known from ancient times and is a deep rich blue made from a ground semi-precious stone, *lapis lazuli.* Artificial ultramarine, also called *French ultramarine,* is the modern replacement and is made of sodium silicate, aluminum, and sulphur—chemicals similar to those in *lapis lazuli.* It is a warm blue, tending toward blue-violet, and one of the most commonly used blues. Although sometimes diluted to give proper consistency for brush work, it is permanent in all forms.

UMBER. See *Burnt Umber* and *Raw Umber.*

UNDERPAINTING. In a painting done in several stages, the underpainting is the first layer after the ground (and after the *imprimatura,* if one is used). The painter plans the underpainting to obtain the variety of effects and optical mixtures he wishes in combination with, or in contrast to, the subsequent overpainted layers of paint, whether they are broken color, glazes, or scumbles. The underpainting can be in *grisaille* (in grays) or in color; it usually is blocked in simply with thin and "lean" paint for better cohesion of the subsequent paint.

UNITY. One of the main interrelating principles of design, unity is achieved through the relationship of the individual parts of the composition to each other and to the whole. In this relationship, monotony is avoided by the use of variety within the unity. Unity appears as a quality of allover self-sufficiency and directed completeness. In order to produce a work of art, these formal means must further the expression of the spiritual content of the painting. See also *Variety*.

V

VALUE. In painting, the term usually refers to the relative lightness or darkness of a tone or color—and indirectly to its luminosity or brilliance. The value of a tone is a gradation somewhere between black and white. A color, to be evaluated, must be transposed into a tonal equivalent before being related to a neutral scale. See also *Color*.

VANDYKE BROWN. Made of native earths containing decomposed vegetable matter as well as asphaltum, this variable pigment is fugitive, a very poor drier, and has all the other defects of asphaltum. Also called *Cassel earth* and *Cologne earth*.

VANISHING POINT. See *Linear Perspective*.

VANITAS. A type of still life. See *Still Life*.

VARIETY. The enhancement of a painting by multiplication and change in the various elements. A certain complexity, giving interest, in which contrasts, conflicts, and juxtapositions contribute to a richness of form and meaning. Variety does not imply chaos. To be effective, it is contained within a certain unity, a vital organization with fitness of the parts to the whole. This is often referred to as "variety in unity" or "unity in variety." See also *Unity*.

VARNISH. A liquid applied to the surface of the painting, which, when dry, forms a clear, hard, but flexible film. *Picture varnish* is the name given varnish when applied as the final protective coat against dirt, soot, fumes, and general wear and tear. *Retouch varnish* is a more diluted form used either as a substitute or temporary final coat when the picture has not fully dried, or as an isolating film between layers of paint. In the latter case, it is brushed over mat or dull areas in order to bring them up to the surrounding gloss and color depth before the application of additional paint; otherwise, the subsequent layers will also "sink in" and become mat. Varnish is added to painting mediums, especially glaze mediums, to give transparency, toughness, and additional adhesiveness. Varnish is used also to isolate layers of paint in mixed-medium techniques, or in mixtures to reduce the absorbency of grounds. Varnishes are made of a resin dissolved in a solvent, which evaporates to leave a thin film. They can be divided into three main groups:
1. The *natural resins* dissolved in solvents, also called the *spirit varnishes*.
   (a) Dammar resin in turpentine; the most serviceable and popular varnish. It forms a hard flexible film that yellows only slightly.
   (b) Mastic resin in turpentine; softer than dammar, it yellows more and has a greater tendency to bloom.
   (c) Shellac dissolved in alcohol; seldom used in permanent painting as it turns dark and cracks with age.
2. The *cooked oil and resin varnishes*.
   (a) Amber Varnish. No longer used. It is doubtful

if any of the so-called amber varnishes contain any true amber.

   (b)   Copal resin melted and cooked with linseed oil and added driers, then thinned with volatile solvents to form the most familiar oil-resin type of varnish. It forms an extremely hard film, exceedingly resistant to the solvent action of thinners. Most authorities feel that copal varnishes are more susceptible to darkening and cracking than dammar or mastic. One variety was called *coach varnish.*

3.   The *synthetic resin varnishes.*

   (a)   Acrylic resins, dissolved in acetone, toluene, and turpentine. In solutions (methacrylate), serving as fixatives and picture varnish.

   (b)   Vinyl resins, dissolved in acetone, toluene, and alcohols. Solutions of polyvinyl acetate (p.v.a) are used as picture varnish.

See also *Resin.*

VEHICLE.   The liquid that is ground with dry color pigment and that carries it to form paint. The term is often used interchangeably with "medium," the ingredient added in the process of painting.

VENETIAN RED.   Originally a native red iron oxide, it is now artificially produced with added calcium sulphate. It is grouped with the so-called "earth colors," and is warmer than Indian red.

VENICE TURPENTINE.   See *Oleoresin.*

VERDIGRIS.   A very old pigment (*vert de Grice,* literally, green of Greece), it is a green, artificially produced from a copper acetate. Poisonous, impermanent, and no longer in use.

VERMILION.   An extremely brilliant, opaque red with a

heavy body, made of mercuric sulphide. A controversial pigment (it sometimes erratically turns black), it has been replaced more or less by the permanent cadmium reds. Made in China since earliest times, the genuine pigment is known as *Chinese vermilion*. In Europe, it was known as *cinnabar*.

VERNISSAGE (vair-nee-SAHZH). (Fr.)   From the word for *varnish,* which was applied supposedly at the last minute, the *vernissage* has come to mean the opening of an exhibition. Or, more properly, the limited pre-opening reception. See *Opening.*

VERSO. (L.)   The back or reverse; as opposed to the front or obverse. See *Recto.*

VERT ÉMERAUDE.   Another name for the green, viridian. Not to be confused with emerald green. See *Viridian.*

VERT PAUL VÉRONÈSE.   See *Emerald Green.*

VIE DE BOHÈME (vee duh boh-EHM). (Fr.)   The romantic life of the Bohemian. See *Bohemian.*

VIGNETTE (vee-NYEHT). (Fr.)   The process or the result of the shading off of a picture into the surrounding ground without a definite bounding line.

VINGT, Les (lay VA*n*). (Fr.) (Also, *Société des Vingt,* The Twenty, and The XX.) A group of twenty painters, including Ensor, who formed an association in Brussels in 1884 to promote and exhibit new and unconventional art. They exhibited each year, and, in addition to their own work, exhibited that of an equal number of invited artists. The Society lasted ten years, during which time the guests included such painters as Cézanne, Gauguin, Monet, Pissarro, Redon, Renoir, Seurat, van Gogh, and Whistler.

VINYL RESIN.   See *Resin* and *Varnish.*

VIRIDIAN. An artificially produced green made of hydrated chromium hydroxide. It is a bright, transparent cool color, probably the most commonly used green, and is permanent. Also called *chromium oxide green transparent, vert émeraude,* and *Guignet's green.*

VIRTUOSO. (It.) Used to describe an artist whose technical facility (paint handling, etc.) is so phenomenal as to far exceed his creative abilities, and to become something in itself. He may also be called "slick" or "commercial."

VIS-À-VIS (vee-zah-VEE). (Fr.) Face to face; opposite.

VISUAL IDIOM. The "language" or characteristic materials of expression used to communicate visually. Each artist has his own individual visual idiom, just as every art form has its own characteristic idiom.

VOLUME. A primary consideration in paintings that contain any illusion of three-dimensional space. Volumes exist in conjunction with three-dimensional negative

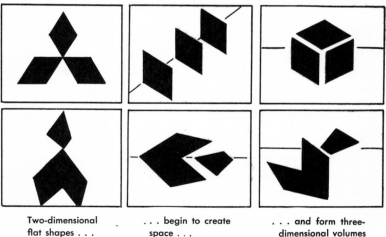

Two-dimensional   . . . begin to create   . . . and form three-
flat shapes . . .   space . . .   dimensional volumes

Examples of a formation of volume.

space. They are positive portions of three-dimensional space occupied by mass—solids enclosed by planes or shapes. The boundaries of volumes are delineated on the picture plane by contours. Once the viewer's sense of being on the surface of the picture plane is, by illusion, changed to a sense of penetration into depth, three-dimensional space and volume are created. One of the major concerns of modern painting is this interrelationship of three-dimensional space and volume to the two-dimensional picture plane. See *Plane* and *Space*.

VOLUME COLOR.   See *Color.*

VOLUMETRIC.   Of or pertaining to volume. See *Volume.*

VORTICISM.   An English variety of Cubism. See *Cubism.*

W

WALL PAINTING.   See *Mural Painting.*

WALNUT OIL.   A drying oil pressed from ground walnuts and used as a binding medium in oil painting. It compares favorably with linseed oil but is not much used, being commercially unprofitable to manufacture.

WARM COLOR.   See *Color.*

WASH.   A term used to describe a thinned, highly fluid color, usually transparent. In oil painting, turpentine is often used to thin a quick-drying preliminary wash. Other washes are thinned with oil and varnish.

WATER COLOR.   Pigment ground in a water vehicle with an added binder such as gum arabic, casein, or dextrin. Other additives are wetting agents, such as oxgall, preservatives, and glycerin. In the technique, the color is used either transparently with washes (aquarelle) or opaquely with body color (gouache, casein, etc.). The support is usually paper of different weights and surfaces, the best being made 100 per cent of rags. See also *Paper*.

WATER-GLASS PAINTING. A seldom used method of painting on plaster (also called mineral painting) in which sodium silicate or potassium silicate is the binder. It has been known as *stereochromy*.

WAX PAINTING. Painting with wax in some form as the medium. It can be either the hot wax (encaustic painting) or the cold wax technique. In the latter, a wax emulsion is used as the medium, with either tempera or linseed oil paints. See *Encaustic Painting*.

WEIGHT. Visual weight is the visual pull or force of attraction of an object or volume, limited by its pictorial, spatial environment. Visual, or compositional weight, de-

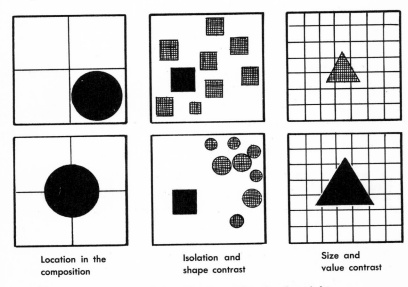

| Location in the composition | Isolation and shape contrast | Size and value contrast |

Examples of differences in visual weight.

pends upon such comparative factors as: location in the composition; extent of isolation—distance from or contrast with other objects; and size, color, and value. Psychological interest (or "eye pull") is another form of attention value and an important factor in weight. Figures, comparably, have more interest than objects; the head and hands of the figure and the eyes in the face are also examples of attention value that increases the visual weight. See also *Balance*.

WET-INTO-WET. See *Mixed Technique*.

WHITE LEAD. See *Flake White*.

WHITING. Native calcium carbonate. It is used in making grounds; and as an extender, especially with glue size, in water-color paints needing body. In poorer grades, it is known as *putty;* in its best, as *Paris white*.

WOOD PANEL. See *Panel*.

Y

YELLOW OCHER. A natural earth color found in a range of shades. It is permanent and has been known from ancient times.

Z

ZEITGEIST (TSYTE-gyste). (Ger.) Time-spirit; the spirit of the age or the times, the general mental and moral climate and its cultural character.

ZINC YELLOW. A pale cool yellow made of zinc chromate. Sometimes called *lemon yellow*. It is not permanent.

ZINC WHITE. A cold white pigment made of pure zinc oxide. It is brilliant but makes a brittle paint film and is an extremely slow drier. In spite of its nontoxic quality and its permanence, it is not always preferable to flake white, except in water techniques, where it is the approved white. Zinc white is also known in water color as *Chinese white.*

BIBLIOGRAPHY

Arnheim, Rudolf. *Art and Visual Perception.* Berkeley and Los Angeles: University of California Press, 1965.

Barnes, Albert C. *The Art in Painting.* New York: Harcourt, Brace and Company, 1937.

Barr, Alfred H. Jr. *Cubism and Abstract Art.* New York: Museum of Modern Art, 1936.

————. *Masters of Modern Art.* New York: Museum of Modern Art, 1958.

Cassirer, Ernst. *An Essay on Man.* New York: Doubleday and Company, 1953.

Chaet, Bernard. *Artists at Work.* Cambridge, Mass.: Webb Books. Distributed by Hill and Wang, New York, 1960.

Cheney, Sheldon. *Expressionism in Art.* New York: Tudor Publishing Company, 1948.

————. *The Story of Modern Art.* New York: Viking Press, 1941.

Cogniat, Raymond. *The Century of the Impressionists.* New York: Crown Publishers, 1960.

Crespelle, Jean-Paul. *The Fauves.* Greenwich, Conn.: New York Graphic Society, 1962.

Delacroix, Eugene. *The Journal of Eugene Delacroix.* Edited and translated from the French by Walter Pach. New York: Crown Publishers, 1948.

Dewey, John. *Art as Experience.* New York: Minton, Balch, and Company, 1934.

Diehl, Gaston. *The Moderns.* New York: Crown Publishers, 1961.

Doerner, Max. *The Materials of the Artist.* New York: Harcourt, Brace and Company, 1940.

Dorival, Bernard. *Twentieth Century Painters.* New York: Universe Books, 1958.

Edman, Irwin. *Arts and the Man.* New York: W. W. Norton and Company, 1939.

Gardener, Helen. *Art Through the Ages.* New York: Harcourt, Brace and Company, 1959.

Ghiselin, Brewster (ed.). *The Creative Process.* New York: The New American Library, 1958.

Gilson, Étienne. *Painting and Reality.* New York: Pantheon Books, 1957.

Gogh, Vincent van. *The Complete Letters of Vincent van Gogh.* Greenwich, Conn.: The New York Graphic Society, 1958.

Goldwater, Robert J., and Marco Treves. *Artists on Art.* New York: Pantheon Books, 1958.

Gombrich, E. H. *Art and Illusion.* New York: Pantheon Books, 1960.

Graves, Maitland. *Color Fundamentals.* New York: McGraw-Hill, 1952.

Haftmann, Werner. *Painting in the Twentieth Century.* New York: Frederick A. Praeger, 1960.

Henri, Robert. *The Art Spirit.* Philadelphia and New York: J. B. Lippincott Co., 1951.

Itten, Johannes. *The Art of Color.* New York: Reinhold Publishers, 1961.

Jackson, Egbert. *Basic Color.* Chicago: Paul Theobald, 1948.

Kay, Reed. *The Painter's Companion.* Cambridge, Mass.: Webb Books. Distributed by Hill and Wang, New York, 1961.

Kepes, Gyorgy. *Language of Vision.* Chicago: Paul Theobald, 1951.

Langer, Susanne K. *Feeling and Form, a Theory of Art Developed from Philosophy in a New Key.* New York: Scribner, 1953.

————. *Philosophy in a New Key.* New York: The New American Library, 1953.

———— (ed.). *Reflections on Art.* Baltimore: Johns Hopkins Press, 1958.

Loran, Erle. *Cézanne's Composition.* Berkeley and Los Angeles: University of California Press, 1950.

Maritain, Jacques. *Creative Intuition in Art and Poetry.* New York: Meridian Books, 1955.

Mayer, Ralph. *The Artist's Handbook of Materials and Techniques.* New York: The Viking Press, 1957.

Moholy-Nagy, László. *The New Vision.* New York: Wittenborn and Company, 1946.

Myers, Bernard S. *Understanding the Arts*. New York: Holt, Rinehart, and Winston, 1963.

Newmann, Thelma. *Plastics as an Art Form*. Philadelphia: Chilton Books, 1965.

Nicolaïdes, Kimon. *The Natural Way to Draw*. Boston: Houghton Mifflin Company, 1941.

Panofsky, Erwin. *Meaning in the Visual Arts*. New York: Doubleday and Company, 1955.

Rader, Melvin M. (ed.). *A Modern Book of Esthetics*. New York: Holt, Rinehart and Winston, 1960.

Rank, Otto. *Art and Artist*. New York: A. A. Knopf, 1932.

Read, Herbert. *The Form of Things Unknown*. New York: Horizon Press, 1960.

Rewald, John. *The History of Impressionism*. New York: The Museum of Modern Art, 1961.

———. *Post-Impressionism, van Gogh to Gauguin*. New York: The Museum of Modern Art, 1961.

Robb, David M., and J. J. Garrison. *Art in the Western World*. New York: Harper Brothers, 1942.

Rosenberg, Harold. *The Anxious Object*. New York: Horizon Press, 1964.

Schneider, Daniel E. *The Psychoanalyst and the Artist*. New York: The New American Library, 1962.

Taubes, Frederic. *The Technique of Oil Painting*. New York: Dodd, Mead, and Company, 1944.

Wilenski, Reginald H. *Modern French Painters*. New York: Harcourt, Brace and World, 1963.

———. *The Modern Movement in Art*. New York: Yoseloff, 1957.

Wölfflin, Heinrich. *Classic Art*. New York: Phaidon Publishers. Distributed by Garden City Books, 1952.

———. *Principles of Art History*. New York: Dover Publications, 1956.